1st EDITION

Perspectives on Diseases and Disorders

Sleep Disorders

Sylvia Engdahl

Book Editor

GALE
CENGAGE Learning

Detroit • New York • San Francisco • New Haven, Conn • Waterville, Maine • London

Christine Nasso, *Publisher*
Elizabeth Des Chenes, *Managing Editor*

For more information, contact:
Greenhaven Press
27500 Drake Rd.
Farmington Hills, MI 48331-3535
Or you can visit our Internet site at gale.cengage.com

For product information and technology assistance, contact us at

Gale Customer Support, 1-800-877-4253
For permission to use material from this text or product, submit all requests online at www.cengage.com/permissions

Further permissions questions can be e-mailed to permissionrequest@cengage.com

Articles in Greenhaven Press anthologies are often edited for length to meet page requirements. In addition, original titles of these works are changed to clearly present the main thesis and to explicitly indicate the author's opinion. Every effort is made to ensure that Greenhaven Press accurately reflects the original intent of the authors. Every effort has been made to trace the owners of copyrighted material.

Cover image copyright © RubberBall/Alamy

LIBRARY OF CONGRESS CATALOGING-IN-PUBLICATION DATA

Sleep disorders / Sylvia Engdahl, book editor.
   p. cm. -- (Perspectives on diseases and disorders)
Includes bibliographical references and index.
ISBN 978-0-7377-5255-7 (hardcover)
1. Sleep disorders--Popular works. I. Engdahl, Sylvia.
RC547.S5188 2011
616.8'498--dc22

2010039236

Printed in the United States of America
2 3 4 5 6 7 15 14 13 12 11

CONTENTS

unfamiliar surroundings, and alcohol or drugs. It usually starts in childhood and increases during the teen years, then declines. Steps should be taken to prevent sleepwalking and to reduce the risk of accidents resulting from it.

CHAPTER **2**   Issues Concerning Sleep Disorders

unrelated to sleep but who turned out to have narcolepsy, a disorder that causes the patient to fall suddenly asleep at inappropriate times or to pass out for no apparent reason. This condition usually begins in adolescence, but doctors often forget to test for it when diagnosing illness.

extremely dangerous, especially for adults. There is an increasing number of reports of people driving cars while sleepwalking without awareness of road conditions or stoplights. It is vital that appropriate precautions be taken in arranging a sleepwalker's nighttime environment.

FOREWORD

"Medicine, to produce health, has to examine disease."
—Plutarch

Independent research on a health issue is often the first
step to complement discussions with a physician. But
locating accurate, well-organized, understandable medical information can be a challenge. A simple Internet search
on terms such as "cancer" or "diabetes," for example, re-
turns an intimidating number of results. Sifting through the
results can be daunting, particularly when some of the information is inconsistent or even contradictory. The Greenhaven Press series Perspectives on Diseases and Disorders
offers a solution to the often overwhelming nature of researching diseases and disorders.

From the clinical to the personal, titles in the Perspectives on Diseases and Disorders series provide students and other researchers with authoritative, accessible
information in unique anthologies that include basic
information about the disease or disorder, controversial
aspects of diagnosis and treatment, and first-person accounts of those impacted by the disease. The result is a
well-rounded combination of primary and secondary
sources that, together, provide the reader with a better
understanding of the disease or disorder.

Each volume in Perspectives on Diseases and Disorders
explores a particular disease or disorder in detail. Material
for each volume is carefully selected from a wide range of
sources, including encyclopedias, journals, newspapers, non-
fiction books, speeches, government documents, pamphlets,
organization newsletters, and position papers. Articles in the
first chapter provide an authoritative, up-to-date over-
view that covers symptoms, causes and effects, treatments,

cures, and medical advances. The second chapter presents a substantial number of opposing viewpoints on controversial treatments and other current debates relating to the volume topic. The third chapter offers a variety of personal perspectives on the disease or disorder. Patients, doctors, caregivers, and loved ones represent just some of the voices found in this narrative chapter.

Each Perspectives on Diseases and Disorders volume also includes:

- An **annotated table of contents** that provides a brief summary of each article in the volume.
- An **introduction** specific to the volume topic.
- Full-color **charts and graphs** to illustrate key points, concepts, and theories.
- Full-color **photos** that show aspects of the disease or disorder and enhance textual material.
- **"Fast Facts"** that highlight pertinent additional statistics and surprising points.
- A **glossary** providing users with definitions of important terms.
- A **chronology** of important dates relating to the disease or disorder.
- An annotated list of **organizations to contact** for students and other readers seeking additional information.
- A **bibliography** of additional books and periodicals for further research.
- A detailed **subject index** that allows readers to quickly find the information they need.

Whether a student researching a disorder, a patient recently diagnosed with a disease, or an individual who simply wants to learn more about a particular disease or disorder, a reader who turns to Perspectives on Diseases and Disorders will find a wealth of information in each volume that offers not only basic information, but also vigorous debate from multiple perspectives.

INTRODUCTION

I n recent decades concern has been growing about the detrimental effects of chronic sleep deprivation. A National Sleep Foundation poll in 2005 found that about three out of four American adults get less sleep than the medically recommended eight hours of sleep per night, and its 2006 poll found the same was true of high school seniors. In 2008 the Centers for Disease Control and Prevention (CDC) reported that about 29 percent of adults sleep less than seven hours per night. At the same time, scientists have been learning that sleeping too little over a long period can cause not only cognitive impairment and depression but medical problems such as heart disease, diabetes, and even obesity.

Most people sleep too little because they are too busy to go to bed early enough and do not realize they are putting themselves at risk by building up a "sleep debt." But there are others who cannot get enough sleep despite a sufficient number of hours in bed, whose sleep is not refreshing, or who have strange and upsetting experiences during sleep. These people—whether they know it or not—have medically recognized sleep disorders. The majority of them do not know it; the National Institutes of Health estimates that 50 percent of sleep disorders remain undiagnosed, and some estimates go as high as 95 percent.

There are a number of reasons why so many victims of sleep disorders do not get treatment. In the first place, often they are not aware that they have a medical condition. They know something is wrong if they have insomnia, but as that frequently results from poor sleep habits or emotional problems, it may be blamed on these even in cases where it has a physiological basis. Less obviously

There are eighty-four types of sleep disorders. (Joe Mcnally/ Time & Life Pictures/ Getty Images)

sleep-related is sleepiness or fatigue during the day despite enough sleep at night, which may be caused by a major sleep disorder such as narcolepsy or sleep apnea that can exist for years without a person's suspecting a sleep problem. And people with disorders that involve bizarre behavior during sleep, or produce experiences such as hallucinations, may be reluctant to seek medical advice for fear that they will be considered crazy—although actually, even violent action while asleep generally does not signify mental illness.

In the second place, because sleep medicine is a new field that was not recognized as a medical specialty until 1996, most doctors have little knowledge of it. Although sleep disorders affect millions of people, specific ones are not common enough for the average doctor to recognize without a more detailed description of symptoms than a patient normally mentions during a routine checkup. Even when sleep disorder victims do seek help, doctors without special training often discount or misdiagnose their problems. This situation is improving as the number of sleep clinics grows and organizations focused on sleep disorders work to educate family physicians on what to look for and how to treat it. But since eighty-four different sleep disorders have so far been identified, it may be a long time before treatment of them all becomes widely accessible.

Diagnosis of a sleep disorder generally requires an overnight stay in a sleep laboratory to be monitored through polysomnography, which means being hooked up to a machine that records a person's physiological processes during sleep. Such testing is not offered everywhere, and even where it is available it requires time and planning. In his book *Sleep*, sleep medicine specialist Carlos H. Schenck writes,

> Every July and August, I know I'm going to get phone calls from parents of soon-to-be college students, wanting to make urgent appointments to have their child evaluated for sleep disorders. What brings young adults in to see us most often at this age are sleepwalking and night terrors. It never really bothered them before, but now that they're going away to college, they're suddenly very worried about what their roommates and dorm-mates will think if they wake up in the middle of the night and do something weird—like wandering naked through the hallway and shouting something about killer clams. . . . They're shocked to hear that there's a two-

month waiting list to be evaluated in the sleep clinic. . . . The time to think about treating a sleep disorder is when they're filling out applications to college, not when they're packing to leave.

Furthermore, opportunity for diagnosis is limited by the fact that overnight sleep studies are extremely expensive—the average cost as of 2010 was over twenty-six hundred dollars—and patients without health insurance that covers such studies often cannot afford them. So even when a doctor recommends seeing a sleep specialist, a firm diagnosis cannot always be made.

Sleep disorders are not life threatening in themselves, except for sleep apnea, which involves pauses in breathing that can be dangerous when severe; however, some sleep disorders do put people at great risk for serious accidents. For example, sleepwalking is harmless—but not when someone sleepwalks out a second-story window or cuts up meat with a kitchen knife or, worse, attempts to drive a car. Similarly, narcolepsy produces a sudden loss of muscle tone that can lead to falls, and the brief attacks of involuntary daytime sleep that occur in untreated narcoleptics can be fatal if they occur while driving.

For that matter, sleepiness resulting from the poor nighttime sleep produced by many lesser disorders, as well as from simply not getting enough hours of sleep, is a major hazard on the road. The sleep medicine website Shift Work Disorder News reports that

> 250,000 drivers fall asleep at the wheel every day, according to the Division of Sleep Medicine at Harvard Medical School. . . . According to the National Highway Traffic Safety Administration, drowsy driving is a factor in more than 100,000 crashes, resulting in 1,550 deaths and 40,000 injuries annually. The National Sleep Foundation puts the numbers much higher: 71,000 injuries and more than 5,500 deaths a year. . . . Researchers have shown that a person who drives after 18 consecutive

hours without sleep performs at the same level as a person with a blood-alcohol concentration of .08% —the legal standard for drunken driving.

Many sleep disorders that do not pose any actual dangers nevertheless affect quality of life. For example, delayed sleep phase syndrome, the inability to sleep or rise as early as social and normal work schedules require, is not viewed as a disorder in someone who is free to set his or her own schedule, but when it interferes with school or work it can make adequate performance impossible and treatment to combat it essential. Parasomnias—disorders such as sleepwalking and sleep terrors that involve abnormal behaviors or experiences during sleep—are at best embarrassing, and in some cases alarming. Sleep paralysis (SP), a condition in which the mind is awake while the body is entering or emerging from the muscular paralysis normal during dreaming, can be scary to someone who is not aware that up to 30 percent of the population experiences it at least once, especially since it is often accompanied by frightening hallucinations that may be interpreted as visitations by ghosts, witches, or aliens. When SP is a manifestation of narcolepsy or occurs frequently for some other reason, it can be treated with medication, but some people prefer to find other ways of dealing with it.

Some sleep problems, such as sleepwalking and night terrors, are common in children but are usually outgrown. Scientists believe that in adults most primary sleep disorders (that is, disorders not attributable to medical or psychiatric conditions or to lifestyle factors) are due to brain abnormalities or damage, some of which may be genetic in origin. Little is known about the underlying causes of the less common ones, the majority of which have been identified and named relatively recently. They are generally treatable but not permanently curable. Research on sleep is now proceeding rapidly, however, and in the future cures for some of these disorders may be found.

CHAPTER **1**

Understanding Sleep Disorders

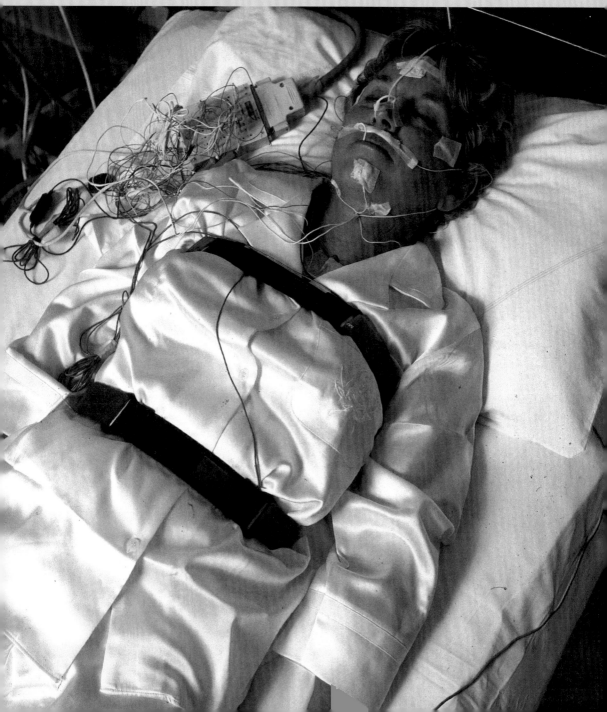

Many Different Sleep Disorders Exist

Rebecca J. Frey et al.

The following article explains what sleep disorders are and describes the most common ones. About a third of all Americans have a sleep disorder at some time in their lives. Dissomnias are disorders involving the amount, restfulness, and timing of sleep, while parasomnias are those in which the patient's behavior is affected by sleep stages or transitions between sleeping and waking. Some sleep disorders are simply outgrown; those that are lifelong can usually be controlled with treatment. The disorders are not fatal in themselves, but insufficient sleep increases a person's risk of depression and of accidents on the road or in the workplace and needs to be remedied. Rebecca Frey and her coauthors are medical writers.

Sleep disorders are a group of syndromes characterized by disturbance in the patient's amount of sleep, quality or timing of sleep, or in behaviors or physiological conditions associated with sleep. There

Photo on facing page. An overnight stay at a sleep laboratory is usually required to diagnose a sleep disorder. (Russell Curtis/ Photo Researchers, Inc.)

SOURCE: Rebecca J. Frey et al. "Sleep Disorders," *Gale Encyclopedia of Medicine,* 3rd edition, Belmont, CA: Gale, 2006. Copyright © 2006 by Gale, a part of Cengage Learning. Reproduced by permission.

are about 81 different sleep disorders, according to the second edition of the *International Classification of Sleep Disorders*. To qualify for the diagnosis of sleep disorder, the condition must be a persistent problem, cause the patient significant emotional distress, and interfere with his or her social or occupational functioning.

Because sleep requirements vary from person to person, there is no specific amount of time spent sleeping that can be used as a cutoff to determine whether a person has a sleep disorder. Some healthy adults need as much as 10 hours of sleep per night whereas others need as little as five hours.

Sleep disorders are a common problem in the general population of North America. Researchers estimate that 20–40% of adults report difficulty sleeping at some point each year. About a third of all Americans will have a sleep disorder at some point in their lives. Twenty percent of adults say that they have problems with chronic insomnia, and 17% consider their sleeping problem to be serious.

As far as is known, sleep disorders are equally common in all racial and ethnic groups in Canada and the United States.

Normal Sleep

Although sleep is a basic behavior in animals as well as humans, researchers still do not completely understand all of its functions in maintaining health. In the past 30 years, however, laboratory studies on human volunteers have yielded new information about the different types of sleep. Increasing interest in sleep disorders led to the recognition of sleep medicine as a distinct medical subspecialty with its own board certification procedures in 1978. Researchers have learned about the cyclical patterns of different types of sleep and their relationships to breathing, heart rate, brain waves, and other physical functions. These measurements are obtained by a technique called polysomnography.

There are five stages of normal human sleep. Four stages consist of non-rapid eye movement (NREM) sleep, with unique brain wave patterns and physical changes occurring. Dreaming occurs in the fifth stage, during rapid eye movement (REM) sleep.

- Stage 1 NREM sleep. This stage occurs while a person is falling asleep. It represents about 5% of a normal adult's sleep time.
- Stage 2 NREM sleep. In this stage, (the beginning of "true" sleep), the person's electroencephalogram (EEG) will show distinctive wave forms called sleep spindles and K complexes. About 50% of sleep time is stage 2 NREM sleep.
- Stages 3 and 4 NREM sleep. Also called delta or slow wave sleep, these are the deepest levels of human sleep and represent 10–20% of sleep time. They usually occur during the first 30–50% of the sleeping period.
- REM sleep. REM sleep accounts for 20–25% of total sleep time. It usually begins about 90 minutes after the person falls asleep, an important measure called REM latency. It alternates with NREM sleep about every hour and a half throughout the night. REM periods increase in length over the course of the night.

Sleep cycles vary with a person's age. Children and adolescents have longer periods of stage 3 and stage 4 NREM sleep than do middle aged or elderly adults. Because of this difference, the doctor will need to take a patient's age into account when evaluating a sleep disorder. Total REM sleep also declines with age.

The average length of nighttime sleep varies among different age groups. Infants typically need about 16 hours of sleep each day, while adolescents need about 9 hours. Most adults sleep between seven and nine hours a night, although pregnant women may need as many as 10 or 11 hours of sleep. This population average appears to be constant throughout the world. In temperate climates, however, people often notice that sleep time varies with the seasons. It is not unusual for people in North America and Europe to sleep about 40 minutes longer per night during the winter.

Sleep disorders are classified based on what causes them. Primary sleep disorders are distinguished from those that are caused by other mental disorders, prescription medications, substance abuse, or medical conditions. The two major categories of primary sleep disorders are the dyssomnias and the parasomnias.

Dyssomnias

Dyssomnias are primary sleep disorders in which the patient suffers from changes in the amount, restfulness, and timing of sleep. The most important dyssomnia is primary insomnia, which is defined as difficulty in falling asleep or remaining asleep that lasts for at least one month. It is estimated that 35% of adults in the United States experience insomnia during any given year, but the number of these adults who are experiencing true primary insomnia is unknown. Primary insomnia can be caused by a traumatic event related to sleep or bedtime, and it is often associated with increased physical or psychological arousal at night. People who experience primary insomnia are often anxious about not being able to sleep. The person may then associate all sleep-related things (their bed, bedtime, etc.) with frustration, making the problem worse. The person then becomes more stressed about not sleeping. Primary insomnia usually begins when the person is a young adult or in middle age.

Hypersomnia is a condition marked by excessive sleepiness during normal waking hours. The patient has either lengthy episodes of daytime sleep or episodes of daytime sleep on a daily basis even though he or she is sleeping normally at night. In some cases, patients with primary hypersomnia have difficulty waking in the morning and may appear confused or angry. This condi-

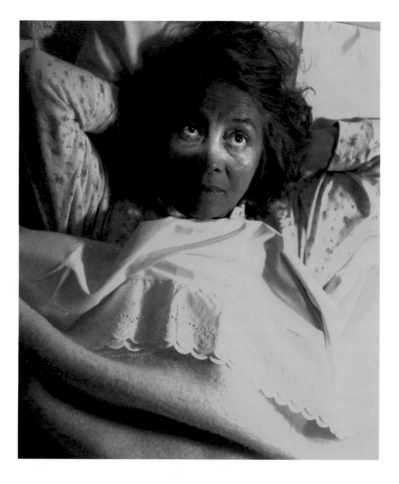

Sleep disorder research indicates that about one-third of Americans will have a sleep disorder in their lifetime. (**Oscar Burriel/ Photo Researchers, Inc.**)

tion is sometimes called sleep drunkenness and is more common in males. The number of people with primary hypersomnia is unknown, although 5–10% of patients in sleep disorder clinics have the disorder. Primary hypersomnia usually affects young adults between the ages of 15 and 30.

Nocturnal myoclonus and restless legs syndrome (RLS) can cause either insomnia or hypersomnia in adults. Patients with nocturnal myoclonus wake up because of cramps or twitches in the calves. These patients feel sleepy the next day. Nocturnal myoclonus is sometimes called periodic limb movement disorder (PLMD). RLS patients have a crawly or aching feeling in their calves that can be relieved by moving or rubbing the legs. RLS often prevents the patient from falling asleep until the early hours of the morning, when the condition is less intense.

Kleine-Levin syndrome is a recurrent form of hypersomnia that affects a person three or four times a year. Doctors do not know the cause of this syndrome. It is marked by two to three days of sleeping 18–20 hours per day, hypersexual behavior, compulsive eating, and irritability. Men are three times more likely than women to have the syndrome. Currently, there is no cure for this disorder.

Narcolepsy is a dyssomnia characterized by recurrent "sleep attacks" that the patient cannot fight. The sleep attacks are about 10–20 minutes long. The patient feels refreshed by the sleep, but typically feels sleepy again several hours later. Narcolepsy has three major symptoms in addition to sleep attacks: cataplexy, hallucinations, and sleep paralysis. Cataplexy is the sudden loss of muscle tone and stability ("drop attacks"). Hallucinations may occur just before falling asleep (hypnagogic) or right after waking up (hypnopompic) and are associated with an episode of REM sleep. Sleep paralysis occurs during the transition from being asleep to waking up. About 40% of patients with narcolepsy have or have had another mental disorder. Although narcolepsy is often regarded as an adult disorder, it has been reported in children as young as three years old. Almost 18% of patients with narcolepsy are 10 years old or younger. It is estimated that 0.02–0.16 of the general population suffer from narcolepsy. Men and women are equally affected.

FAST FACT

An estimated 50 to 95 percent of sleep disorder cases are undiagnosed.

Breathing-Related Sleep Disorders

Breathing-related sleep disorders are syndromes in which the patient's sleep is interrupted by problems with his or her breathing. There are three types of breathing-related sleep disorders:

- Obstructive sleep apnea syndrome. This is the most common form of breathing-related sleep disorder, marked by episodes of blockage in the upper airway during sleep. It is found primarily in obese people. Patients with this disorder typically alternate between periods of snoring or gasping (when their airway is partly open) and periods of silence (when their airway is blocked). Very loud snoring is a clue to this disorder.
- Central sleep apnea syndrome. This disorder is primarily found in elderly patients with heart or neurological conditions that affect their ability to breathe properly. It is not associated with airway blockage and may be related to brain disease.
- Central alveolar hypoventilation syndrome. This disorder is found most often in extremely obese people. The patient's airway is not blocked, but his or her blood oxygen level is too low.
- Mixed-type sleep apnea syndrome. This disorder combines symptoms of both obstructive and central sleep apnea.

Circadian rhythm sleep disorders are dyssomnias resulting from a discrepancy between the person's daily sleep/wake patterns and demands of social activities, shift work, or travel. The term *circadian* comes from a Latin word meaning daily. There are three circadian rhythm sleep disorders. Delayed sleep phase type is characterized by going to bed and arising later than most people. Jet lag type is caused by travel to a new time zone. Shift work type is caused by the schedule of a person's job. People who are ordinarily early risers appear to be more vulnerable to jet lag and shift work-related circadian rhythm disorders than people who are "night owls." There are some patients who do not fit the pattern of these three disorders and appear to be the opposite of the delayed sleep phase type. These patients have an advanced sleep phase pattern and cannot stay awake in the evening, but wake up on their own in the early morning.

Parasomnias

Parasomnias are primary sleep disorders in which the patient's behavior is affected by specific sleep stages or transitions between sleeping and waking. They are sometimes described as disorders of physiological arousal during sleep.

Nightmare disorder is a parasomnia in which the patient is repeatedly awakened from sleep by frightening dreams and is fully alert on awakening. The actual rate of occurrence of nightmare disorder is unknown. Approximately 10–50% of children between three and five years old have nightmares. They occur during REM sleep, usually in the second half of the night. The child is usually able to remember the content of the nightmare and may be afraid to go back to sleep. More females than males have this disorder, but it is not known whether the sex difference reflects a difference in occurrence or a difference in reporting. Nightmare disorder is most likely to occur in children or adults under severe or traumatic stress.

Sleep terror disorder is a parasomnia in which the patient awakens screaming or crying. The patient also has physical signs of arousal, like sweating, shaking, etc. It is sometimes referred to as pavor nocturnus. Unlike nightmares, sleep terrors typically occur in stage 3 or stage 4 NREM sleep during the first third of the night. The patient may be confused or disoriented for several minutes and cannot recall the content of the dream. He or she may fall asleep again and not remember the episode the next morning. Sleep terror disorder is most common in children four to 12 years old and is outgrown in adolescence. It affects about 3% of children. Fewer than 1% of adults have the disorder. In adults, it usually begins between the ages of 20 and 30. In children, more males than females have the disorder. In adults, men and women are equally affected.

Risk Factors for Sleep Disorders

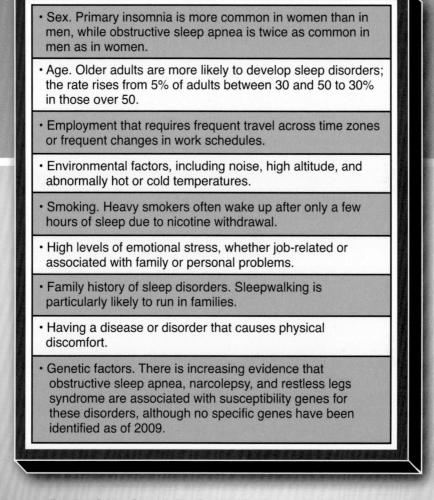

- Sex. Primary insomnia is more common in women than in men, while obstructive sleep apnea is twice as common in men as in women.

- Age. Older adults are more likely to develop sleep disorders; the rate rises from 5% of adults between 30 and 50 to 30% in those over 50.

- Employment that requires frequent travel across time zones or frequent changes in work schedules.

- Environmental factors, including noise, high altitude, and abnormally hot or cold temperatures.

- Smoking. Heavy smokers often wake up after only a few hours of sleep due to nicotine withdrawal.

- High levels of emotional stress, whether job-related or associated with family or personal problems.

- Family history of sleep disorders. Sleepwalking is particularly likely to run in families.

- Having a disease or disorder that causes physical discomfort.

- Genetic factors. There is increasing evidence that obstructive sleep apnea, narcolepsy, and restless legs syndrome are associated with susceptibility genes for these disorders, although no specific genes have been identified as of 2009.

Taken from: Rebecca Frey, et al. "Sleep Disorders," *Gale Encyclopedia of Medicine*, 2009.

Sleepwalking disorder, which is sometimes called somnambulism, occurs when the patient is capable of complex movements during sleep, including walking. Like sleep terror disorder, sleepwalking occurs during stage 3 and stage 4 NREM sleep during the first part of the night. If the patient is awakened during a sleepwalking episode, he or she may be disoriented and have no memory of the behavior. In addition to walking around, patients with sleepwalking disorder have been reported to eat, use the bathroom, unlock doors, or talk to others. It is estimated that 10–30% of children have at least one episode of sleepwalking. However, only 1–5% meet the criteria for sleepwalking disorder. The disorder is most common in children eight to 12 years old. It is unusual for sleepwalking to occur for the first time in adults.

Unlike sleepwalking, REM sleep behavior disorder occurs later in the night and the patient can remember what they were dreaming. The physical activities of the patient are often violent.

Sleep Disorders Related to Other Conditions

In addition to the primary sleep disorders, there are three categories of sleep disorders that are caused by or related to substance use or other physical or mental disorders.

Many mental disorders, especially depression or one of the anxiety disorders, can cause sleep disturbances. Psychiatric disorders are the most common cause of chronic insomnia.

Some patients with chronic neurological conditions like Parkinson's disease or Huntington's disease may develop sleep disorders. Sleep disorders have also been associated with viral encephalitis, brain disease, and hypo- or hyperthyroidism.

The use of drugs, alcohol, and caffeine frequently produces disturbances in sleep patterns. Alcohol abuse is associated with insomnia. The person may initially feel sleepy after drinking, but wakes up or sleeps fitfully during the second half of the night. Alcohol can also increase the severity of breathing-related sleep disorders. With amphetamines or cocaine, the patient typically suffers from insomnia during drug use and hypersomnia during drug withdrawal. Opioids usually make short-term users sleepy. However, long-term users develop tolerance and may suffer from insomnia.

In addition to alcohol and drugs that are abused, a variety of prescription medications can affect sleep patterns. These medications include antihistamines, corticosteroids, asthma medicines, and drugs that affect the central nervous system.

Pediatricians estimate that 20–30% of children have difficulties with sleep that are serious enough to disturb their families. Although sleepwalking and night terror disorder occur more frequently in children than in adults, children can also suffer from narcolepsy and sleep apnea syndrome. . . .

Symptoms and Diagnosis

The most important symptoms of sleep disorders are insomnia and sleepiness during waking hours. Insomnia is by far the more common of the two symptoms. It covers a number of different patterns of sleep disturbance. These patterns include inability to fall asleep at bedtime, repeated awakening during the night, and/or inability to go back to sleep once awakened.

Diagnosis of sleep disorders usually requires a psychological history as well as a medical history. The patient's sex and age are useful starting points in assessing the problem. The doctor may also talk to other family members in order to obtain information about the patient's symptoms. The family's observations are particularly important to evaluate sleepwalking, kicking in bed, snoring loudly, or other behaviors that the patient cannot remember. . . .

Laboratory Sleep Studies

If the doctor is considering breathing-related sleep disorders, myoclonus, or narcolepsy as possible diagnoses, he or she may ask the patient to be tested in a sleep laboratory or at home with portable instruments.

Polysomnography can be used to help diagnose sleep disorders as well as conduct research into sleep. In some cases the patient is tested in a special sleep laboratory. The advantage of this testing is the availability and expertise of trained technologists, but it is expensive. As of 2009, however, portable equipment is available for home recording of certain specific physiological functions.

The multiple sleep latency test (MSLT) is frequently used to measure the severity of the patient's daytime sleepiness. The test measures sleep latency (the speed with which the patient falls asleep) during a series of planned naps during the day. The test also measures the amount of REM sleep that occurs. Two or more episodes of REM sleep under these conditions indicates narcolepsy. This test can also be used to help diagnose primary hypersomnia.

The repeated test of sustained wakefulness (RTSW) is a test that measures sleep latency by challenging the patient's ability to stay awake. In the RTSW, the patient is placed in a quiet room with dim lighting and is asked to stay awake. As with the MSLT, the testing pattern is repeated at intervals during the day. . . .

Prognosis

The prognosis depends on the specific disorder. Children usually outgrow sleep disorders. Patients with Kleine-Levin syndrome usually get better around age 40. Narcolepsy, however, is a lifelong disorder, although cataplexy can be successfully controlled with medication, and many people find that their symptoms naturally decrease after age 60. The prognosis for sleep disorders related to other conditions depends on successful treatment of the substance abuse, medical condition, or other mental disorder. The prognosis for primary sleep disorders is affected by many things, including the patient's age, sex, occupation, personality characteristics, family circumstances, neighborhood environment, and similar factors.

About 85% of people with insomnia find relief with a combination of sleep hygiene and medication. Although there is no cure for sleep apnea, treatment can reduce the associated risks of high blood pressure and heart disease.

Insomnia and other sleep disorders are not fatal in and of themselves; however, chronic insomnia is associated with an increased risk of depression and suicide. In addition, insufficient sleep increases a person's risk of accidents on the road and in the workplace, with the possibility of serious injury or death. Driver fatigue is responsible for an estimated 100,000 motor vehicle accidents and 1500 deaths each year in the United States, according to the National Highway Traffic Safety Administration.

Poor Sleep Has a Significant Impact on Health and Quality of Life

Richard Scott

In the following article Richard Scott points out that three out of four American adults get less sleep than is recommended, 40 million of whom suffer from chronic sleep disorders. People tend to minimize their sleep problems, say sleep specialists; yet sleep deprivation has damaging effects on mental functioning, mood, and motor skills as well as on the organs, cardiovascular system, brain, and even the immune system. In young children it causes learning difficulties, and some sleep disorders increase risk for metabolic syndrome, which affects the heart. Major sleep disorders have a great impact on a person's quality of life. Scott is the managing editor of Case in Point, *a magazine for professionals in the case management profession.*

As the world continues to take on the always-open qualities of an all-night cafe, where the lights may dim but never shut off, the amount of time that Americans devote to sleep is growing less and less.

SOURCE: Richard Scott, "Awake at Night: The Ill Effects of Poor Sleep and Sleep Disorders," *Case in Point,* December 2007, pp. 29–32. Reproduced by permission.

A 2005 poll conducted by the National Sleep Foundation found that slightly more than 25 percent of American adults sleep for the recommended baseline of eight hours per night. In other words, three-quarters of the adult population gets less sleep than the scientific community recommends. And the number of people who get less than six hours of sleep a night is on the rise, with the figures creeping incrementally from 12 percent of the population in 1998 to 16 percent in 2005.

The National Sleep Foundation's latest poll, which focused on the sleeping habits of women, found that, in brief, American women do not sleep well. At least not well enough to meet the recommendations of leading organizations, including those suggested by the National Institutes of Health and the National Sleep Foundation itself.

Sixty-seven percent of women, according to the findings from the 2007 Sleep in America Poll, experience sleep problems at least a few nights per week. That figure includes 72 percent of working mothers and 68 percent of single, working women who reported symptoms of a sleep problem, such as insomnia.

In fact, more than 40 million Americans suffer from chronic, long-term sleep disorders every year, while an additional 20 million experience sleep problems occasionally, according to the National Institute of Neurological Disorders and Stroke (NINDS). The ramifications on the overall health and lifestyle habits of the bleary-eyed have proven costly. Sleep disorders, while accounting for an estimated $16 billion in annual medical costs (a figure that does not include indirect costs due to lost productivity), take a toll on other areas, such as work, driving, relationships, and even cardiovascular health and weight.

Sleep Is Essential to Health

Insomnia, sleep apnea, restless legs syndrome and narcolepsy are the four most common disorders that affect the

The Stages of Sleep

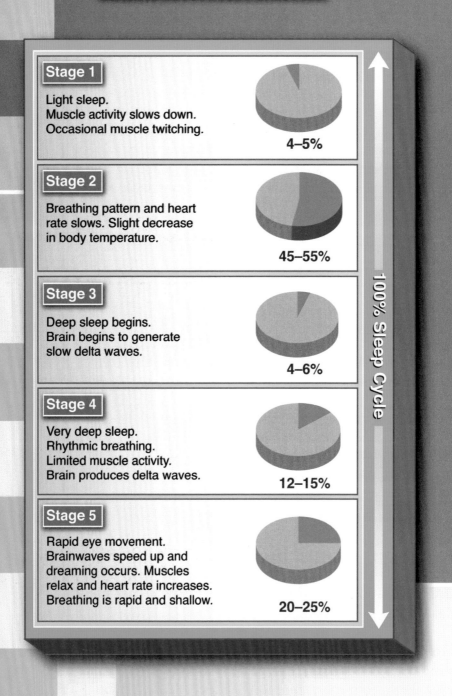

Stage 1

Light sleep.
Muscle activity slows down.
Occasional muscle twitching.

4–5%

Stage 2

Breathing pattern and heart
rate slows. Slight decrease
in body temperature.

45–55%

Stage 3

Deep sleep begins.
Brain begins to generate
slow delta waves.

4–6%

Stage 4

Very deep sleep.
Rhythmic breathing.
Limited muscle activity.
Brain produces delta waves.

12–15%

Stage 5

Rapid eye movement.
Brainwaves speed up and
dreaming occurs. Muscles
relax and heart rate increases.
Breathing is rapid and shallow.

20–25%

100% Sleep Cycle

Taken from: Doctors Medical Center, www.doctorsmedicalcenter.org. 2000 Vale Rd. San Pablo, CA 94806
(510) 970-5000.

sleep and the consequent day-after malaise and malfunctioning of millions of Americans. As the scientific study of sleep continues to expand, so too do the number of identifiable sleep disorders. The American Academy of Sleep Medicine cites 81 official disorders, though some of them, like sleep talking, are relatively innocuous, while others, like exploding head syndrome, are exceedingly rare. But regardless of the source of disruption, inadequate sleep usually correlates to inadequate health.

"People tend to minimize their sleep problems," says Clete A. Kushida, MD, PhD, an associate professor at Stanford University's Department of Psychiatry and Behavioral Science. "They forget that one-third of their life is spent asleep; in addition to the focus on things like exercise and nutrition, sleep is vitally important."

Dr. Kushida points to cognitive functioning, mood and motor skills as three areas that fall under "the constellation of effects" that occur as a result of sleep deprivation. He also cites deleterious effects on our organ systems, the cardiovascular system and the brain. Studies have shown that sleep deprivation causes our nervous systems to work improperly and our memory and concentration to become impaired, while others suggest that it affects the immune system in detrimental ways.

It used to be that the mystery surrounding sleep was whether or not it was an important activity. A common rationale as to the importance of sleep goes like this: From the terms of an evolutionary standpoint, if we are intended to spend one-third of our days in an inert—and defenseless—position of sleep, then it must serve an indispensable function for human survival.

Animal studies have shown it to do just that. Studying rats, which have a normal lifespan of two to three years, researchers found that those kept severely deprived of sleep survived an average of only three weeks. The rats

> **FAST FACT**
>
> Sleep did not become a medical specialty until 1978 and was not covered in medical schools until the 1980s.

developed abnormally low body temperatures, skyrocketing metabolic rates and sores on their tail and paws suggestive of a deficient immune system.

Today, the mystery about sleep is not whether it is important, but what, precisely, it does.

Sleep Deprivation Has Serious Effects

"In humans," Dr. Kushida says, "the data is fairly mixed as to what the actual function of sleep is. There are various hypotheses. But we do know that if a person is sleep deprived, if they have problems such as excessive daytime sleepiness, it puts them at risk for motor vehicle as well as work-related accidents. They have difficulties with their cognitive functions. Their ability to think unimpaired is affected, as well as their mood changes."

A recent study from England, which for 17 years monitored the sleep patterns and the residual health of 10,000 government workers, found that those who obtained an

Sleep-deprived people have difficulty staying awake at work, and their cognitive abilities are curtailed. (© David Young-Wolff/Alamy)

average of less than five hours of sleep per night were more than twice as likely to die of heart disease, and faced a 1.7-fold increased risk of death from all causes.

Statistics on the population of children are equally disturbing. A study published in a recent issue of *Sleep* shows that children as young as the preschool age face learning difficulties, including problems with visual and spatial processing, when they get less than adequate sleep. Another study published in the *American Journal of Respiratory & Critical Care Medicine* found that teenagers with sleep apnea are nearly seven times more likely to develop metabolic syndrome, a group of risk factors for type 2 diabetes, heart disease and stroke that include abdominal obesity, high blood pressure, elevated blood sugar and dangerous cholesterol levels. The fragmentation of sleep, adds Dr. Kushida, can also interrupt childhood development by interfering with growth hormone secretion.

"I want to emphasize that if a person has sleep problems that are affecting their quality of life or their ability to obtain restful sleep at night, it is important to have it evaluated by a sleep specialist or a primary care physician," advises Dr. Kushida. "There's no question that the major sleep disorders have a great impact on a person's quality of life."

The Importance of Sleep to Adolescent Health Is Often Underestimated

David S. Reitman

In the following article David S. Reitman explains that the importance of adequate sleep to adolescents' health is often underestimated, although lack of sleep can lead to many serious problems. He then describes the cases of three of his teenage patients, two of whom turned out to have sleep disorders—delayed sleep phase syndrome and obstructive sleep apnea—and one whose sleep difficulty was caused by depression. All of them overcame their problems through treatment. Reitman is an adolescent medicine specialist in Washington, D.C. He is chairman of pediatrics at Suburban Hospital in Bethesda, Maryland.

S leep is an important, yet frequently underestimated component of adolescent health. Adequate sleep is essential for achieving maximal cognitive abilities as well as for maintaining the energy needed to meet the demands of a busy adolescent's schedule. Lack of quality

SOURCE: David S. Reitman, "Identifying Sleep-Related Problems in Teens," *Consultant for Pediatricians,* February 2009, p. 57. Copyright © 2009 United Business Media LLC. Reproduced by permission.

sleep can result in attention problems, cognitive dulling, various somatic [body-related] complaints (such as headaches and abdominal pain), and mood disturbances. . . .

Why Sleep?

Sleep involves a complex series of physiological events that evolve throughout the lifespan. Various conflicting theories describe how the brain balances its need for sleep with its need for wakefulness. I like to use a model in which 2 parallel processes control the sleep-wake cycle. The first process involves biological homeostasis [stability]: the brain maintains an innate balance between sleep and wakefulness that is reset every morning when the person wakes up. As the day progresses, this homeostatic drive accumulates a "sleep need" that, by bedtime, compels the person to sleep and then resets the balance for the next morning. The second process involves a brain-based circadian [24-hour] rhythm that controls the production of melatonin, cortisol, and other sleep-controlling hormones.

While pre-adolescents require 10 to 11 hours of sleep at night, adolescents entering puberty have a sleep requirement of 9 to 9½ hours. Coincident with the decreased need for sleep is an approximately 2-hour physiological diurnal [daily] sleep phase delay (involving changes in both the homeostatic drive and melatonin secretion). Thus, a pre-teen who needed to go to bed by 9 or 10 at night might, as an adolescent, not experience the urge to sleep until 11 or 12.

One can see how external factors such as school, activities, sports, and after-school jobs can contribute to a chronic lack of sleep in adolescence. For example, many middle schools and high schools start their academic days at about 7:30 A.M., which can result in students getting 6 to 7 hours of sleep, with subsequent sleep deprivation in many. Contrary to the beliefs of many parents and teens, the notion that one can "catch up on sleep" by sleeping

Preadolescents require ten to eleven hours of sleep, and pubescent adolescents require nine to nine and one-half hours. (David Grossman/Photo Researchers, Inc.)

until noon on the weekends is incorrect, and trying to do so may exacerbate sleep problems. From a sleep hygiene perspective, a relatively consistent sleep pattern is best.

Adolescent medicine providers frequently are asked to determine whether a teenager's sleeping pattern is normal or suggestive of a sleep disorder. Some of the sleep problems commonly seen in adolescence include nightmares, nocturnal enuresis [bed wetting], and decreased sleep resulting from over-enrollment in activities. However, an adolescent's physician must also be alert to the possibility of more severe disorders, such as sleep phase disorders, parasomnias (eg, sleepwalking), obstructive sleep apnea syndrome, and narcolepsy.

The following three scenarios illustrate some of the more common adolescent sleep problems, and the accompanying discussions may provide insight into the sorts of issues you are likely to encounter.

Case 1: Fatigue Subsequent to Difficulty Falling Asleep at Night

Chris, 16 years of age, comes to the office in mid-September complaining of persistent daytime fatigue. His mother says that she has to drag him out of bed in the morning and remarks that since school began 4 weeks ago, he "just can't get his act together" on school days. Teachers are concerned that Chris is falling asleep in class and is unable to function well academically this year. After school, he has soccer practice. He sometimes takes a 2-hour nap between 6 and 8 P.M. so that he has the energy needed to do his homework at night. Weekends tend to be less problematic because Chris can sleep until 12 or 1 in the afternoon.

The physical examination findings are unremarkable. Chris denies any new stresses or anxieties. When asked about his summer, he reports that he had a great summer and that he stayed up almost every night until 3 A.M. using the computer and talking to friends. The fatigue became a problem only when he had to start getting up for school at 6 A.M. In response to the suggestion that he needs to get into bed by 10 P.M. with all extraneous stimuli, such as cell phone and computer, turned off, Chris counters that despite consistent attempts to go to bed earlier, he "just lies in bed until 3 A.M., so why bother going to bed earlier?" . . .

Delayed Sleep Phase Syndrome

Chris likely suffers from delayed sleep phase syndrome (DSPS). DSPS frequently occurs after long periods in which the sleep-wake cycle is delayed by more than 2 hours, such as during summer vacations. Although sleep onset is delayed, the sleep quality tends to be normal (as evidenced by polysomnography [a sleep study]). However, the teenager who cannot readjust to a normal sleep routine, as is required by a school schedule, will eventually demonstrate signs and symptoms of sleep deprivation.

These may include headaches, daytime fatigue, irritability, emotional lability, and cognitive/ attentional deficits.

Which interventions will most effectively reset a diurnal schedule depend on the amount of time between the desired and actual sleep onset times. When sleep onset is less than 2 hours later than the desired bedtime (a bedtime that would provide the ideal 9 hours of sleep), then one can simply attempt to advance both the bedtime and the wake time by approximately 15 minutes every night until the bedtime and sleep onset time coincide. For example, if a patient cannot fall asleep until 1 A.M. but has been sleeping until 10 A.M., you can recommend that the bedtime be advanced to 12:45 A.M., then 12:30 A.M., then 12:15 A.M., and so forth, with concurrent wake times of 9:45, 9:30, and 9:15 A.M., until the desired sleep schedule is reached. Ideally, I would recommend beginning this process at least 1 week before the start of a new school year or job. For the duration of this treatment, napping should be minimized to 30 minutes a day at most.

FAST FACT

A 2009 study published in the journal *Sleep* found that adolescents with a childhood diagnosis of attention deficit/ hyperactivity disorder (ADHD) are more likely to have current and lifetime sleep problems and disorders, whether or not they still have ADHD symptoms.

However, patients such as Chris, whose sleep onset is 3 hours (or more) later than the desired sleep time, probably need to undergo home-based chronotherapy. This treatment is time- and labor-intensive for the family, but it has been shown to be effective in treating DSPS. It involves progressively delaying the sleep phase by 3 hours per night until the desired bedtime is reached. Thus, I would instruct Chris and his family to delay bedtime (and wake time) by approximately 3 hours every day. He would need to keep himself up until 6 A.M., 9 A.M., 12 P.M., and so forth, and would have to wake up at 3 P.M., 6 P.M., 9 P.M., respectively. During this therapy, napping is forbidden and stimulant drinks should be avoided. Once he reaches the desired schedule, Chris must maintain the schedule (give or take 30 minutes) on weekends to avoid a relapse.

Phototherapy is another effective treatment for DSPS. However, it tends to be a more complicated intervention and is beyond the scope of this article. If chronotherapy fails and phototherapy is required, I generally refer the patient to a sleep disorder specialist. . . .

Outcome of this case: Chris underwent chronotherapy with the support of his parents. After 4 or 5 days, he had adjusted to a schedule in which he went to sleep at 10:30 P.M. and awoke at 6 A.M. From the end of September through December, his school performance was improved. Unfortunately, during the 2-week winter vacation he began once again habitually staying up late and sleeping until 1 P.M.

Thus, 3 days before he had to go back to school, Chris and his parents needed to repeat chronotherapy to get him back on an appropriate schedule.

Case 2: Headaches and Unrefreshing Sleep in a Snorer

Fourteen-year-old Trevor, who has been extremely healthy, comes in for an annual athletic physical. Although he insists that he has no physical complaints, his mother interjects, "Trevor, I thought you wanted to tell the doctor about your headaches! Doctor, he complains at least 4 or 5 times a week that his head hurts, and he is always tired. Last week, he missed the bus twice because it was so hard to get him out of bed. Oh, and while we are on this subject, is there any pill you can give him to make him stop snoring? My room is across the hall, and I can't sleep unless I keep my head under a pillow!"

Speaking privately with his physician, Trevor sheepishly admits that he has been feeling tired a lot lately and that he often takes a 2-hour nap in the afternoon; however, the naps don't make him feel less tired. He goes to sleep exhausted at 10 P.M. and sleeps until 7 A.M., but he doesn't feel refreshed in the morning. If he sleeps until 10 or 11 A.M. on the weekends, he feels a little bit better but still needs an afternoon nap. Trevor admits he has headaches, which usually occur in the afternoon. He denies visual changes, photophobia [excessive sensitivity to light], and vomiting with the headaches. The headaches are usually bilateral and "squeezing" in quality.

Not ADHD

Trevor denies any other physical complaints, symptoms of depression, and drug use. His grades have not been as good over the past year because he has a hard time concentrating in school, and his teachers have recommended that he be evaluated for attention-deficit/hyperactivity disorder (ADHD).

The results of a comprehensive physical examination, including neurological examination, are normal.

In the past, many clinicians might have counseled Trevor and his mother that teenagers are always tired and that feeling tired is part of being an adolescent. However, this scenario has certain features that are more troubling. First, Trevor appears consistently fatigued even when he gets 9 or more hours of sleep at night. Even a substantial afternoon nap does not seem to help him feel better. Another notable feature is that his teachers have noticed an objective, gradual decline in his academic abilities, to the degree that they want him evaluated for ADHD.

Obstructive Sleep Apnea

Might Trevor have a syndrome of sleep-disordered breathing, such as obstructive sleep apnea (OSA)? Patients with this condition frequently have difficulties with air inspiration during sleep. . . . This frequently results in increased wakefulness that disrupts healthy sleep architecture. While patients may not be aware of these symptoms, they will experience symptoms of sleep deprivation. . . .

In this case, the historical feature that piques my interest the most is the patient's snoring. His loud snoring bothers Trevor's mother so much that she wants medication to fix it! It would be important to ask family

The Most Common Sleep Disorders

Name of disorder	What it is	Who has it
Primary Insomnia	Difficulty in getting to sleep or staying asleep without a known cause.	10% of population chronic; 30%–50% occasional (estimate vary).
Obstructive Sleep Apnea (OSA) **Central Sleep Apnea**	Episodic cessation of breathing during sleep, leading to frequent brief pauses.	More than 12 million is US; most common in older men.
Narcolepsy	Sudden daytime sleep attacks, often accompanied by other symptoms.	About 50,000 known in US; estimated 150,000—2.4 million undiagnosed.
Delayed Sleep Phase Syndrome Advanced Sleep Phase Syndrome	Inability to sleep during the hours most people do.	Fairly common; not a disorder unless it interferes with work or school schedules.
Restless Legs Syndrome (RLS)	Sensations in the legs relieved only by movement; often interferes with sleep.	Estimated 2 million in US; most common in older adults.
Sleep Bruxism	Involuntary grinding or clenching of teeth while sleeping.	Estimated 8%–10% of population.
Sleep Paralysis (a symptom of narcolepsy) **Isolated Sleep Paralysis** (no narcolepsy)	Awareness of paralysis at sleep onset or while waking, often accompanied by hypnagogic/hypnopompic hallucinations.	Common; not a disorder unless frequent or accompanied by narcolepsy.
Sleep Terrors (pavor nocturnus) Also called **Night Terrors**	Waking in the night screaming or crying, shaking, and sweating, usually without later recall. Not the same as nightmares.	About 3% of children aged 4–12; fewer than 1% of adults.
Sleepwalking (somnambulism)	Walking or other activity during sleep with no memory of it after waking.	Estimated 1%–15% of population; most common in childhood.

[Compiled by editor.]

members about the quality of the snoring: How loud is it? Is it rhythmic or disjointed sounding? Does it ever sound like Trevor stops breathing for a period, followed by a gasping breathing pattern?

While many used to believe that OSA only occurred in overweight and obese persons, we now know that this is not the case. The American Academy of Pediatrics recommends that pediatricians screen all children and adolescents for a significant history of snoring and that they consider polysomnography (sleep study) in those who snore—regardless of body habitus [physique]—to evaluate for sleep apnea. In many persons, such as Trevor, upper airway obstruction can be caused solely by anatomical abnormalities, such as large tonsils or adenoids.

Outcome of this case: Trevor underwent polysomnography, which demonstrated multiple obstructive apneic [interrupted breathing] episodes throughout the night, occasionally with oxygen desaturations into the mid-80s (%), clinching the diagnosis of OSA. He was referred to an otolaryngologist who eventually removed his tonsils. His snoring almost immediately disappeared, and a follow-up sleep study demonstrated complete resolution of the apneic events. Moreover, Trevor's energy and grades dramatically improved.

It should be noted that surgical corrections for OSA are not universally effective. The gold-standard treatment is continuous positive airway pressure (CPAP) [a device worn while sleeping], specially for the more "classic" obese patient with OSA. However, many children and adolescents do not tolerate CPAP administration and may elect a surgical option if one is appropriate.

Case 3: Low Energy, Loss of Appetite, and Difficulty in Sleeping

Fifteen-year-old Melanie just finished her freshman year in high school. She comes to the office to have a tuberculin skin test and physical clearance for a job at a summer camp. You notice that she looks tired, and she admits that she has been having trouble sleeping. Melanie relates that she tries to go to sleep as early as 9 P.M., but she usually lies in bed, thinking about her life, for at least 2 to 3 hours. She sets her alarm for 7 A.M., but often spontaneously wakes up as early as 5 A.M. (or even earlier) and cannot fall back asleep. She denies any new stresses that might be keeping her awake, but she does relate that almost 1 year ago, her best friend was killed in a car accident (Melanie was in the car) and that she has been thinking about the incident a lot.

Melanie admits that she feels guilty that she survived the accident while her friend did not. She states that over the past few months, her energy levels have dwindled and that she "just does not have the energy to go out with her friends." She spends a lot of time by herself in her room, writing poetry. Her mother has been concerned that she is losing weight, and she admits that she has a poor appetite. She wishes that she could get back to feeling the way she used to.

She denies any drug, alcohol, or caffeinated beverage use. When told, "It must be really difficult to have all this going on inside. You're dealing with so much at once, no wonder you can't sleep," Melanie starts to cry.

Research regarding adolescent emotional health has demonstrated bidirectional relationships between emotional state and the quality of sleep. Children and adolescents with anxiety disorders, depression, and bipolar disorders frequently have difficulty establishing and maintaining sleep on a regular basis. Conversely, teenagers who are sleep-deprived frequently report mood disturbances. Although attempts to determine the true cause in a given patient may seem futile—turning up little more than a classic "chicken-and-egg" situation [i.e., which is the cause and which the effect?]—it is also possible (and even likely) that poor-quality sleep and poor emotional health concurrently worsen each other.

Psychiatric Disorders

When evaluating patients with sleep problems, always screen for psychiatric problems. Anxiety disorders frequently cause insomnia, with increased time to fall asleep and difficulty reaching deep sleep. Theoretically, a sense of security is needed to achieve a deep sleep. The absence of that degree of security precludes the ability to achieve deep and restful sleep, thus giving the anxious adolescent chronic complaints of fatigue and insomnia.

Melanie demonstrates features consistent with major depressive disorder (MDD): more than 2 weeks of depressed mood, anhedonia [inability to feel pleasure], sleep disturbance, loss of appetite, feelings of guilt and worthlessness, and lack of energy. Other signs and symptoms that would be consistent with MDD include decreased concentration, psychomotor retardation (or agitation), and suicidal ideation. . . .

Outcome of this case: Melanie denied any suicidal intentions, and she promised to immediately tell her mother if she began to have suicidal thoughts. She was referred to an adolescent psychiatrist who, after a comprehensive evaluation, diagnosed MDD and initiated therapy with a selective serotonin reuptake inhibitor [antidepressant drug]. She also began counseling with a psychologist who specialized in depression and grief. After 3 to 4 weeks, her mood and her sleep patterns gradually began to improve. About 2 months later, Melanie's mother reported that her daughter was "getting back to her old self."

Obstructive Sleep Apnea Is a Serious Problem

Chris Meagher

The following article is Chris Meagher's report of a night he spent in a sleep laboratory as a subject for a sleep study. He describes what it was like to have a polysomnogram, a procedure during which a person's brain waves and breathing are monitored all night. From the investigators he learned about sleep disorders, especially obstructive sleep apnea, which causes a person to repeatedly stop breathing during sleep. Apnea has recently been found to be a serious problem, which was not realized until sleep study technology became available. The disorder can be successfully treated, but many sufferers are unaware that they have it. Meagher is a reporter for the *Santa Barbara Independent* in Santa Barbara, California.

M y roommate snores. Until a couple weeks ago, I discounted it as an annoyance and occasional—okay, often—interruption of sleep. Now, after having participated in a polysomnogram, a sleep study if you will, I think there may be more to his nighttime noise-making; I think he has obstructive sleep apnea.

When word went around the office that a subject was needed for a sleep study, I pounced on the opportunity. When the day came, I packed my overnight bag, grabbed my favorite pillow, and headed to the Arete Sleep Health Sleep Lab, where I met Mansoor Hussain, the lab supervisor for the three Arete sleep labs on the South Coast [of Santa Barbara County]. The newly renovated Arete in Santa Barbara used to be known as the Sleep Disorder Center of Santa Barbara and sees three to five patients every day of the week. I didn't think I had any sleep problems going in, but I was still a little nervous to discover what the study might find.

Wired for Sleep

The sleep lab resembles any doctor's office—a waiting room, thousands of files stacked behind the receptionist, and four or five private rooms tucked into the corners of the hall. Unlike other doctor's offices, however, the treatment rooms at Arete don't have uncomfortable plastic table beds draped with butcher paper, but rather cozy-looking double beds, a nightstand, and a television.

FAST FACT

In a 2003 study of professional football players, linemen with the largest neck circumference and highest body mass index accounted for 85 percent of cases of sleep-disordered breathing.

After I changed into my sleepwear, Hussain brought me to the information station, a room with several televisions and computers where patients are monitored by technicians throughout the night. There I got geared up for the evening, with Hussain attaching various wires and sensors to my face, head, shoulders, and legs, as well as my chest and abdomen. He also placed small little tubes in my nose to register my breathing patterns. It sounds like it might be uncomfortable, and it did take some time to get used to having wires come out of my head, but overall it wasn't too bad. Hussain and I headed back to my room, which was also outfitted with a couple cameras so the staff could watch me twist and turn through the night. Hussain left me to watch a little television before drifting off to sleep.

While I wasn't completely comfortable with my surroundings, and I went to bed a little earlier than normal, I fell asleep readily enough and awoke feeling like I'd slept pretty much as I normally do, which, according to the study, isn't particularly abnormal. The results did enlighten me to some of my nighttime quirks. One of the most interesting pieces of information I got from the study is I sleep on my back. I always thought I slept on my sides, never on my back. But for more than two hours that Friday night, I slept on my back and when I did, my apnea level increased to 7.8 events per hour.

Out of Breath

Apnea events lasting longer than 10 seconds are considered significant, but many usually last from 20 to 30 seconds and some can last longer than a minute. The apnea episode usually ends when the patient wakes up because they can't breathe, and the body's "arousal" response allows the person's airway to reopen. Even though the body wakes up, the person usually doesn't remember it, which is one reason people don't realize they even have sleep apnea. Like my roommate, people have little to no idea there may be a problem unless someone tells them. If the apnea is serious enough, it doesn't matter if a person sleeps for one hour or 12, they won't feel well-rested when they wake up.

My longest bout of apnea lasted 19 seconds. Scary, right? Hold your breath and count to 19 seconds and tell me this isn't a scary fact. I didn't know how to react to the fact that at points during my sleep that night I was not breathing. Luckily, the events were few and far between—only 3.1 per hour—not nearly enough to be considered abnormal.

What is abnormal, Dr. Charles Curatalo—a registered Santa Barbara sleep doctor—told me, is when people have breathing pauses between 30 and 100 times per hour for up to a minute. This, as one might imagine, leads to almost no deep sleep. While doctors still haven't figured out why we sleep, there's no question that we need it. We spend one-third of our lives under the covers, and studies have shown sleep is important for the state of the brain as well as the functionality of our immune systems, among other things.

Some doctors believe the rapid eye movement (REM) stage of sleep, when the brain is in a very active state, is used for memory consolidation. But not getting sleep clearly causes impairment, Curatalo said. Aggravated headaches in the morning are common in those who can't sleep, and a person's memory, concentration, and mood are all affected. According to some studies, people with sleep apnea are twice as likely to get into a traffic accident. There is almost certainly a direct correlation between a person's weight and having sleep apnea. Chances are greatly increased that a person with a body mass index higher than 30 (normal would be between 18 and 25) has sleep apnea. A large neck often will weigh on the throat to the point where the person's breathing tract is blocked. . . .

Eyes Wide Shut

There are 79 kinds of sleep disorders affecting more than 70 million Americans—many of whom don't even know they have a problem. Between 80 and 90 percent of people with obstructive sleep apnea are undiagnosed; the average patient goes seven years before being diagnosed.

The seriousness of sleep apnea has gone from the academic world to the real world, explained Jeff Barr, a South Coast territory manager with Arete. As technology has picked up in the last 30 years, so has the medical community's awareness of just how big a problem sleep

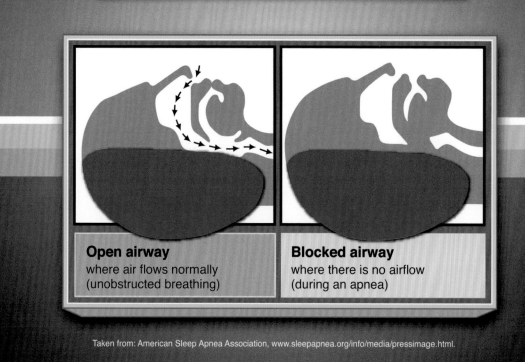

Airway Blocked During Sleep Apnea

Open airway
where air flows normally
(unobstructed breathing)

Blocked airway
where there is no airflow
(during an apnea)

Taken from: American Sleep Apnea Association, www.sleepapnea.org/info/media/pressimage.html.

apnea can be. "Nobody took it seriously until there was a way to clearly replicate a night's sleep and document the disorders," Barr said. Another problem, said another Arete South Coast territory manager, Summer Battle, is getting the word out to doctors to question their patients regarding their sleep habits. According to a 2002 article in *American Family Physician* by three doctors in Israel, when physicians ask patients about snoring, excessive sleepiness during the day, and reports of apneic events, the number of diagnosed and treated cases increases eightfold. "If you stopped breathing during the day you would run to your doctor," said Battle. "But when people are sleeping they don't know."

So how is apnea, the most prevalent of sleep disorders, treated? Before I hit the hay for the night, Hussain fit me for a CPAP (Continuous Positive Airway Pressure)

Sleep apnea is treated with a continuous positive airway pressure machine, which allows air to move freely into the lungs by covering the nose and forcing the throat open. **(Veronique Burger/Photo Researchers, Inc.)**

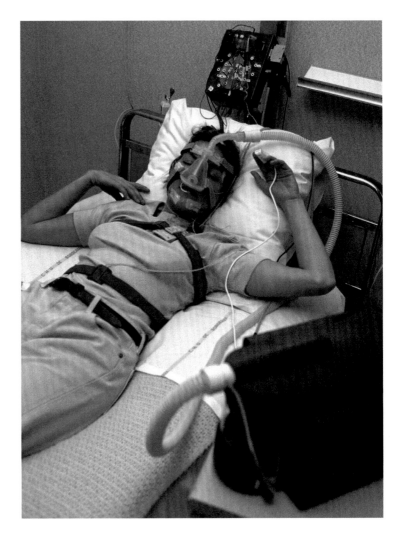

machine, a little mask that covered my nose and forced my throat open, leaving a way for airflow to move freely. If Hussain or his technician had diagnosed any potential sleep apnea that night after two hours, they would've hooked me up with the machine. After the sleep study, people are diagnosed by a doctor as to whether they could benefit from CPAP therapy, which, along with the sleep study, is often covered by insurance. There are many shapes and sizes to a CPAP, which now are made to be nearly silent and can fit into a travel bag. While it takes some getting used to, the CPAP can change the way a person sleeps. Many apnea sufferers haven't experienced a good night's sleep in years, but after one night using the CPAP they feel more rested than they have in a long time.

Sleeping and Eating

Getting treated for sleep apnea can also help people lose weight. Sleep apnea can alter certain hunger-inducing hormones, tricking them into believing the body is hungry. The body doesn't tell a person with sleep apnea that they're full, and they end up eating more, leading to weight gain. Once the apnea is treated, the artificial need to eat is eliminated. So, getting treated for sleep apnea doesn't just mean you'll get a good night's sleep, but also that you can expect to see a reduction in blood pressure and a lessened risk of stroke and heart disease.

However, according to those at Arete, 50 percent of the national apnea sufferers can't get used to the CPAP and throw it into the closet. (At Arete, initial meetings with respiratory therapists are arranged along with follow-up meetings, and compliance by Arete patients is at about 90 percent.)

I met with Curatalo—who has more than 16 years' experience treating sleep disorders—the week after my sleep study, and I was informed by the good doctor that I have no clinical sleep disorder. (I did, however, learn lots of interesting tidbits from my information-packed report. For instance, I only spent 10.7 percent of my time in bed in REM stage sleep, while generally a person would spend 20–25 percent in the dream state.)

But I was armed with all sorts of information to take home to my roommate, as well as the idea of how the treatment of sleep apnea can make a world of difference. "You really are changing the life of the patient," Hussain said. Now if I could only convince my roommate to let Arete help him, maybe we both could get a good night's sleep for once.

Delayed Sleep Phase Disorder Is a Common Cause of Teen Insomnia

John Cline

In the following article John Cline explains a condition called delayed sleep phase disorder. (This condition is more commonly known as delayed sleep phase syndrome; it is not considered a disorder unless it interferes with a person's activity schedule.) This condition exists when the person's circadian rhythm or biological "clock" is set differently from average, so that he or she is unable to sleep during the normal hours and must go to bed very late and get up late in order to get sufficient sleep. In cases where school or work requires early rising it creates a serious problem, but the biological "clock" can be reset through treatment. Cline is a clinical psychologist, a diplomate of the American Board of Sleep Medicine, and a professor at Yale University.

Kristin was running late again. Could she possibly make it to school on time? Her school has a very strict morning start time and she had often missed it. If she is late, not only will she be locked out of her first period class, but she could be suspended this time. She's al-

SOURCE: John Cline, "Sleepless in America: Delayed Sleep Phase, Parts 1 and 2," *Psychology Today*, August 30 and September 24, 2009. Copyright © 2009 Sussex Publishers LLC. Reproduced by permission.

ready had several warnings and fears this could be her last. Why had she stayed up so late last night texting her friends?

Kristin has been having a hard time getting to school on time because she doesn't go to bed until 3 A.M. This is not because she has a hard time falling asleep once she gets in bed. She does not have insomnia. She only has trouble falling asleep if she goes to bed before 3 A.M. At 3 A.M. she is able to easily fall asleep. She does not find it easy, however, to get up at 6:30 A.M., which is the last possible time she can get up and still make it to school on time. In fact, her mother and father practically have to pull her out of bed to get her up. When she does make it to school on time, she often falls asleep during her morning classes. By the time of her afternoon classes, she finally seems to wake up. She is tired all the time and can be irritable. Her grades have suffered as well. On the weekends she still goes to bed around 3 A.M. but sleeps until 1 or 2 P.M. The weekends are the only time she feels rested. She dreads Sunday night knowing what will happen Monday morning.

A Common Disorder Among Teens

The sleep problem Kristin is having is one of the circadian [24-hour] rhythm sleep disorders and one that is very common among young people. Circadian rhythm sleep disorders often lead to poor sleep among teens. . . . The primary feature of the Circadian Rhythm Sleep Disorder, Delayed Sleep Phase Type (Delayed Sleep Phase Disorder) is that the major sleep episode is delayed as compared to the desired clock time. That is, the bedtime is at a notably later time than the "normal" time to retire. Instead of sleeping from, say, 10:30 P.M. to 6:30 A.M., the person with delayed sleep phase may sleep, as in Kristin's case, from 3:00 A.M. until whenever she is forced to get up. This can lead to problems such as difficulty falling asleep if trying to go to bed at an earlier time; insufficient sleep if having to get up earlier than the delayed morning rise time; and extreme difficulty waking up when necessary due to social demands such as school or work.

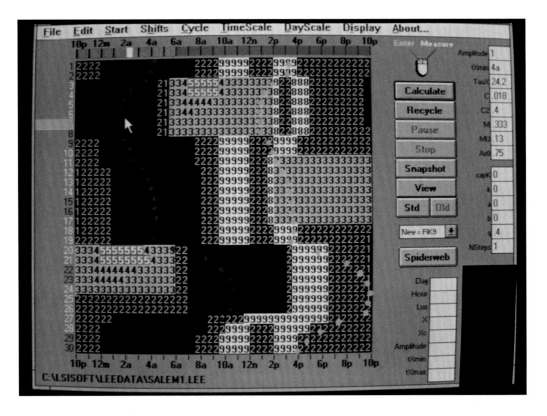

A computer display shows a person's circadian rhythm profile, which will be used to help diagnose the patient's particular sleep disorder.
(Hank Morgan/Photo Researchers, Inc.)

With a Delayed Sleep Phase Disorder, the person's bed time is usually delayed until after 2 A.M. and may be as late as 6 A.M. Adequate functioning is very difficult during the day if the person has to get up at regular times for work or school. Often there is heavy use of alcohol or sleeping medication in an effort to initiate sleep at an earlier time. The sleep architecture is generally normal if the person is allowed to keep an uninterrupted sleep schedule. This means that the stages of sleep are about the same as someone sleeping on a "normal" schedule, just at a different time of the day.

Resetting the Biological Clock

This disorder often starts gradually and leads to a "resetting" of the circadian (24 hour) biological "clock." It often develops as the person stays up later working on a computer, texting friends who also have sleep problems, playing video games or watching TV. Not only do these activities keep the person up but they expose the eye to a significant amount of light later and later in the day. The circadian clock is most strongly set or "entrained" by light. The presence of bright light is a signal for humans to be awake, just as it is in other diurnal animals. For us, darkness is the signal to sleep. Historically there was not much light after the sun went down and sleep generally came easy. Today we can have very bright light sources impinging on our retinas at any time of the day and this can easily, to our detriment, shift the circadian clock.

While the prevalence of delayed sleep phase disorder is currently unknown, it is clearly more common among adolescents and young adults. Among these young people, the prevalence is reported to be 7% to 16%. About 10% of patients that present to sleep disorders clinics with a complaint of chronic insomnia have a Delayed Sleep Phase Disorder. . . .

Seeing a Sleep Specialist

[Kristin] had to meet with the principal. The message was clear: take care of this problem or you will fail and not graduate with your class. After discussing this problem with her parents, she agreed to see her pediatrician who recommended an evaluation with a behavioral sleep specialist. The diagnosis was clear. Kristin has delayed sleep phase disorder. A letter was sent to the principal asking for a temporary later start time for school while she was working on her sleep problem. This request was granted by giving her a study hall in the morning with prior approval to miss this class if necessary. This reduced her stress considerably and helped her better focus on her school work and on the sleep program.

The sleep specialist recommended immediately limiting use of the computer and sending text messages to

FAST FACT

A study conducted by researchers at the Eastern Virginia Medical School found that earlier starting times for schools are associated with increased teen car accidents.

friends to no later than 9 P.M. Not wanting to fail this school year, she reluctantly agreed. Her parents obtained a recommended bright light box that she would start using every morning upon awakening. She started taking an over the counter supplement of melatonin, although the sleep specialist noted that this is not an FDA approved treatment and over the counter supplements are not closely regulated by the government. She also kept a sleep journal, started going to bed 15 minutes earlier every few days and used a very loud alarm to get out of bed in the morning. Although it was difficult, over a period of a number weeks she was able to "reset" her circadian clock. She eventually was going to bed around 11:00 P.M. and was able to get herself up at 6:30 A.M. She still tended to sleep a bit later on the weekends but maintained a regular 11 P.M. bed time most nights of the week, including weekends. This took some ongoing effort on her part. She almost never missed her morning study hall. She finished the school year with reasonable grades and graduated with her class.

Treatment for Delayed Sleep Phase Disorder

Kristin's treatment highlights a number of the techniques used to "reset" the circadian clock and end the nightmare of delayed sleep phase disorder.

Some of these techniques, such as keeping a sleep journal, gradually going to bed earlier and not looking into bright light sources like computers late at night can be used by anyone who finds that they are going to bed and getting up later and later. Other techniques such as phototherapy, oral melatonin and chronotherapy should be used under the direction of a sleep specialist or a physician familiar with these techniques. This is because careful attention must be paid to the timing of these interventions so as to not make sleep problems worse. Calculating the appropriate times requires sound knowledge of the sleep/wake cycle and circadian rhythms. . . .

Distribution of Human Chronotypes

Chronotype depends on whether a person prefers to go to sleep early and get up early, or to go to sleep later in the night and get up late. Larks are early types, owls are late types.

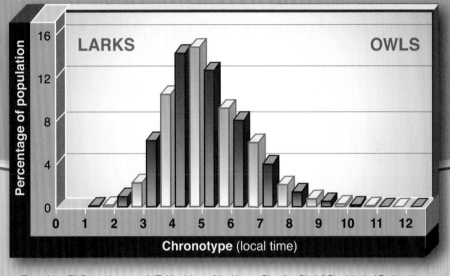

Taken from: Till Roenneberge et al. "Epidemiology of the Human Circadian Clock," *Physiological Review* 11: 429–438 (2007).

Often people with this problem will use sleeping pills or alcohol to try and get to sleep sooner but this rarely works. Alcohol usually makes the problem worse. It is still unclear to what degree both genetic and environmental factors impact on the development of this disorder but both are most likely involved. People with this disorder may experience depressed mood and have great difficulty functioning at school or work. A delayed sleep phase occurs when people are habitually going to bed later and getting up later than the desired clock time. (An advanced sleep phase, often seen in the elderly, is the opposite. The bed time and rise times occur earlier in the day than is normative.) People with delayed sleep phase disorder typically go to sleep between 2:00 and 6:00 A.M. Delayed sleep phase disorder may last from months to decades, usually starts in adolescence and rarely starts after age 30.

Sleepwalking Usually Peaks During Adolescence

Betsy Bates

In the following article Betsy Bates explains why people with a predisposition to sleepwalking are especially vulnerable to it in adolescence, although it often first emerges in the preteen years. The disorder can be aggravated by sleep deprivation, sleeping in unfamiliar surroundings, and alcohol or drugs. There are similarities between sleepwalking and sleep terrors that are common in childhood; both are disorders of delta stage (deep) sleep, from which arousing a person is difficult, and in both cases the person has no memory of the event afterward. Sleepwalkers are often highly agitated and take actions that are dangerous, so it is important to make the environment in which susceptible teenagers sleep as safe as possible. Bates is a medical journalist.

Sleepwalking peaks in adolescence, and it's no wonder, Dr. Rafael Pelayo said at a pediatric update sponsored by Stanford University.

A disorder of arousal in delta (non-REM) sleep, sleepwalking coincides with growth spurts. It can be ex-

SOURCE: Betsy Bates, "Adolescent Sleepwalkers Are Often Agitated," *Pediatric News*, November 2007, pp. 44–46. Copyright © 2007 International Medical News Group. Reproduced by permission.

acerbated by sleep deprivation, sleeping in unfamiliar surroundings, and alcohol, as well as other drugs, said Dr. Pelayo, a pediatric neurologist and director of the pediatric sleep service at the university.

Picture a college student who crashes in a friend's dorm room after overimbibing at the end of a week of studying late for midterms. The scenario sets the stage for sleepwalking, characterized by increased slow-wave sleep, particularly between stage 3 and stage 4 sleep in the first third of the night.

About 5 to 10 percent of children sleepwalk, but by adulthood roughly half have stopped. (Martin Lladé/ Gaia Moments/Alamy)

"Anything that throws you off the transition can make you more vulnerable to sleepwalk if you're predisposed to sleepwalking to begin with," Dr. Pelayo said.

Often, it's easy to predict which teenagers will sleepwalk. They may have a family history of sleep disorders, including sleepwalking, and they are likely to have had sleep terrors in early childhood.

Looking back, their parents may see similarities between the "blood-curdling screams" and dissociative state they remember from childhood sleep terrors and the zombie-like condition of a sleepwalker.

Arousal is difficult or impossible in both disorders, and the child or teen is likely to awaken refreshed and

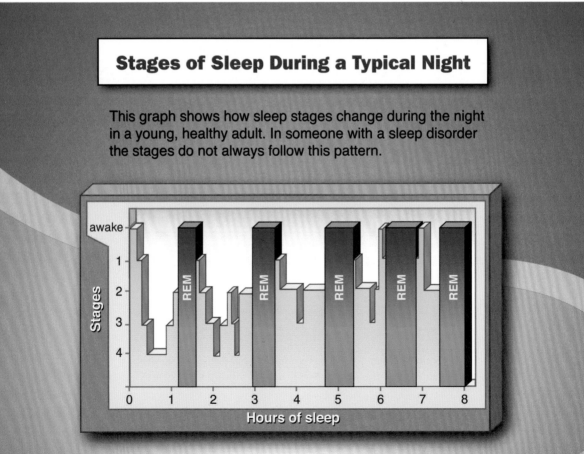

Stages of Sleep During a Typical Night

This graph shows how sleep stages change during the night in a young, healthy adult. In someone with a sleep disorder the stages do not always follow this pattern.

Taken from: National Institutes of Health, *Sleep, Sleep Disorders, and Biological Rhythms*, 2003, NIH Publication 04–4989.

amnesic [unremembering] to the events (although their parents may feel sleep deprived!).

The first sleepwalking episode often emerges in a school-aged child during a night of catch-up sleep following sleep deprivation because of a slumber party, a late-night family event, or jet lag.

Incidence rises during adolescence, and then declines. About 5%–10% of children sleepwalk, but roughly half of them stop before they reach adulthood.

Like a child immersed in a night terror, an adolescent sleepwalker is agitated, bearing no resemblance to the peaceful amblers sometimes depicted in movies or sitcoms. "They don't really walk. They kind of sleep-flee. They're trying to run away," explained Dr. Pelayo.

Sleepwalking Can Be Frightening

Like night terror behavior, sleepwalking can be bizarre, even frightening. Sleepwalkers may seem frantic, their movements wild, their voices altered. They have an altered sense of pain. They may lash out if someone tries to restrain them.

Literally, they may try to escape, walking out the door of the house and starting the car, or, if highly agitated, shoving a fist through a window. "Anything you can do . . . automatically, with your eyes closed you can do sleepwalking," said Dr. Pelayo. "They can turn on power tools," he said.

Later, if they have any memory of the event at all, it will be merely a vague sense that something was odd during the night.

Observers might be quite shaken by a sleepwalker's behavior. "You can imagine people thinking something supernatural is going on. I tell you this, because your patients will have this in the back of their minds. You might as well bring this up," said Dr. Pelayo.

It may help to explain that some dissociation is a part of normal sleep, hardwired into human beings as a defense mechanism. At the end of 90 minutes (60 minutes for infants), all human beings open their eyes briefly, make sure everything is OK, and then fall back asleep, without remembering the episodes later: "If you slept 8 hours in a row, don't you think predators would have picked you off?"

Similarly, everyone begins the night in stage 1 REM [rapid eye movement] sleep, believing they are awake when they are asleep.

The phenomenon occurs every day at medical conferences, Dr. Pelayo said pointedly, when someone's eyes close and head nods. Perhaps he emits a soft snore. Yet, if you poke him, he sits up abruptly and insists, "I'm awake. I'm resting my eyes."

"As a general principle, we can all say what time we went to bed. None of us remembers the moment we fell asleep," Dr. Pelayo commented.

Sleepwalkers simply have an altered threshold for awakening during sleep transitions, leading to behavior miscues in the brain.

"We can make any child sleepwalk. Take any child who's asleep, get him on his feet, and make him walk to the bathroom, urinate, and come back. That's sleepwalking. The next day the child is not going to remember this at all," he said.

Although sleepwalking is far more common, partial complex seizures can look similar and should be considered as a differential diagnosis, cautioned Dr. Pelayo. Seizures occur during any time of the night, not just the first third, typically during transitions from REM to non-REM sleep.

Suspicions should be raised in an older teen "sleepwalking" for the first time.

Such a patient should receive a sleep-deprived EEG [electroencephalogram] to rule out a seizure disorder, Dr. Pelayo recommended.

FAST FACT

Sleepwalkers are not acting out dreams. Dreaming occurs during REM sleep, whereas sleepwalking occurs during non-REM sleep.

Safety Is First Priority in Management

Contrary to long-held myths, it is not harmful to sleep-walkers to try to wake them up.

It is, however, generally pointless, and may be dangerous to the person attempting to intervene in the strange behaviors associated with the common parasomnia, said Dr. Pelayo. "The bottom line with sleepwalkers is they can hurt themselves." Therefore, the first management principle is "safety, safety, safety," not only for the sleep-walker, but for observers.

He offered these steps to reducing harm associated with sleepwalking:

- Prevent the behavior. Warn the parents of children with night terrors that they may become sleepwalkers. Particularly in these vulnerable children, avoid sleep deprivation and conditions that may foster sleep fragmentation, such as untreated obstructive sleep apnea or alcohol use.
- Interrupt the cycle. Instruct parents to awaken sleep-walkers 15 minutes after they have fallen fully asleep. If parents wait too long, the child may already be in stage 3 sleep, and an awakening can induce sleep-walking rather than preventing it. An awakening in stage 2 sleep can push the sleepwalker into a deeper level of stage 4 sleep, avoiding a sleepwalking episode.
- Safety-proof the environment. Advise parents to take apart bunk beds and to cover windows with draperies to minimize injury if a child tries to punch his or her way out of a room. Ask whether there are weapons in the home (including knives), and, if so, make sure they are locked up safely during the night. Car keys also should be inaccessible.
- Make sure parents have a heads-up. Suggest installing buzzers on exterior doors so parents know if a teenager has exited. In cold climates, sleepwalkers have been known to develop frostbite during outdoor excursions.

- Caution against overreaction. Parents have been known to tie up children who sleepwalk, or to lock them into rooms.
- Do something simple. Having the child sleep in a sleeping bag may be enough to prevent wandering.
- Consider donazepam 0.5–2.0 mg, as needed. This muscle relaxant raises the arousal threshold for sleepwalkers and may be useful.

CHAPTER 2

Issues Concerning Sleep Disorders

Medication for Insomnia Usually Does More Harm than Good

Jerry Siegel

In the following viewpoint Jerry Siegel argues that prescription drugs for insomnia do not produce a state of "natural" sleep, but act on many types of cells in the body, often working at cross purposes. According to studies, he says, people with insomnia do not have shortened life spans compared with people who sleep normally, but the long-term use of sleeping pills may reduce life span. Sleeping pills can also cause depression, memory problems, falls, aggressiveness, confusion, and even sleepwalking. In Siegel's opinion, nondrug treatments of insomnia can be more effective than medication and do not involve the risks. Siegel is a professor of psychiatry at the University of California–Los Angeles and chief of neurobiology research for the Veterans Administration's Greater Los Angeles Healthcare Service.

Pharmacists in the United States filled more than 56 million prescriptions for sleeping pills in 2008 at a cost of $4.5 billion, a startling 70 percent increase from 2002. They are among the most advertised, most prescribed and most profitable drugs. Although many

Photo on previous page. Teen drug and alcohol abuse can cause or mask symptoms of sleep disorders. (© imagegallery/Alamy)

SOURCE: Jerry Siegel, "Are Sleeping Pills Good for You?" *Huffington Post*, February 4, 2010. Reproduced by permission of the author.

prescriptions are given for short term use of about two weeks, two-thirds of all sleeping pills are consumed by chronic users who have taken hypnotics for an average of five years or more. Recently developed sleeping pills, including Lunesta (eszopiclone) and Ambien CR (zolpidem) are being promoted as effective for long term use. They have been demonstrated to produce on average a 10–30 minute increase in total daily sleep time for up to six months, not a very large effect. But are these pills good for you?

Most sleeping pills (e.g., Valium, Ambien, Lunesta, Sonata) act on the benzodiazepine site or "receptor" in cell membranes. When these drugs attach to this site, they mimic the effect of GABA, a ubiquitous brain chemical that decreases the activity of most brain cells. Contrary to some drug company claims, drugs acting on the benzodiazepine receptor do not "zero in" on and selectively decrease the activity of wake promoting neurons. Brain cells related to waking contain these receptors, but so do brain cells related to sleep, to heart and blood pressure control, sensory perception, motor control and the regulation of internal functions. The sleep inducing effect of sleeping pills is a result of the simultaneous inhibition caused by benzodiazepine receptors in all of these cell types, often working at cross purposes with regard to sleep. The state induced is not "natural" sleep.

Most sleeping pills are taken to relieve insomnia. According to several epidemiological studies, people with insomnia either do not have any marked shortening of lifespan relative to those reporting normal sleep or actually have a somewhat increased lifespan.

Many cases of insomnia are linked to depression. However, studies in which insomnia subjects were randomly assigned to either placebo or benzodiazepine

FAST FACT

A national survey revealed that over 1.6 million American adults use some form of complementary and alternative medicine to treat insomnia or for trouble sleeping, according to the National Center for Complementary and Alternative Medicine, part of the National Institutes of Health.

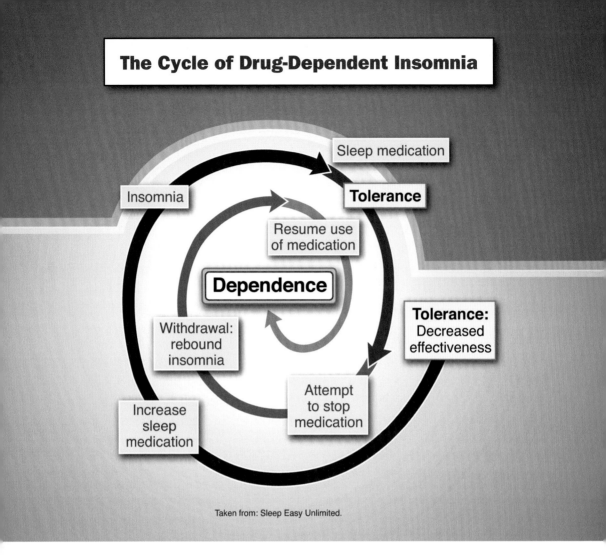

The Cycle of Drug-Dependent Insomnia

Sleep medication

Tolerance

Insomnia

Resume use
of medication

Dependence

Withdrawal:
rebound
insomnia

Tolerance:
Decreased
effectiveness

Increase
sleep
medication

Attempt
to stop
medication

Taken from: Sleep Easy Unlimited.

sleeping pills, reported that the rate of depression was doubled in those who took sleeping pills. Suicide rates are increased in those who had taken hypnotic medications. Benzodiazepines were reported to have caused 3.8 percent of all deaths by drug overdose. Other troubling consequences of sleeping pill use are memory problems, falls, aggressiveness, and confusion. Sleepwalking, sleep eating and driving while not fully awake are common side effects. Those taking sleeping pills can be expected to feel a short term relief from insomnia when they first begin taking the pills. However, short term usage frequently leads to chronic usage and dependence.

Long Term Use May Reduce Lifespan

The most troubling consequence of chronic sleeping pill usage is an apparent reduction in lifespan in chronic sleeping pills users relative to those reporting equivalent insomnia who did not take sleeping pills. Chronic sleeping pill use might be roughly comparable to cigarette smoking in its effect on lifespan. The life shortening effect of chronic sleeping pill usage has now been reported in at least 12 studies published in respected peer reviewed publications. Two studies have reported no effect of hypnotic usage on lifespan. No study has reported any lifespan or overall health benefit of chronic sleeping pill usage, which is striking considering that so much of the research on sleeping pills is funded by the drug companies producing them.

Despite the random assignment controls of some of the studies reporting adverse effect of sleeping pill usage, it remains possible that subjects staying in studies with benzodiazepine agonist use are inherently predisposed to die or develop certain diseases sooner, and that the pills are not the cause. At one point a similar argument was made for cigarette smoking, i.e. it was claimed that people inclined to smoke have a higher risk of lung cancer, but that this risk was not due to smoking. This contention was thoroughly disproved with the help of animal studies where all variables can be controlled. Such studies have not yet been done for hypnotic drugs.

How could these drugs cause the adverse effects that have been reported? In addition to their presence on a wide variety of brain cells controlling bodily systems, benzodiazepine receptors also exist in large numbers in bodily organs including the heart, gall bladder, urinary bladder, thyroid, liver, lung, stomach, testes, pancreas and kidneys and are activated by many commonly used sleeping pills. Benzodiazepine receptors are present on red blood cells, on tumors, as well as on cells of the immune system. Increased rates of infection have been reported with the use of hypnotics.

Sleeping pill use has been linked to cancer as well as cardiac death. In the periphery and to a lesser extent within the brain, activation of the benzodiazepine site directly affects the mitochondria, the cell's energy machine which is involved in inflammation, cholesterol transport, adaptation to stress and cell death. When sleeping pills that attach to this receptor are taken at night, all of the benzodiazepine receptors are activated for hours, fol-

Sleeping pills can cause depression, memory problems, aggressiveness, falls, confusion, and sleepwalking. Chronic use may even reduce a person's life span. (Olivier Voisin/Photo Researchers, Inc.)

lowed by withdrawal during the day. This cycle of activation-withdrawal of all of the brain and body's benzodiazepine receptors never happens in undrugged individuals.

Non-drug Treatment of Insomnia Can Be Effective

Insomnia can be a devastating problem. In those cases where depression, chronic anxiety, pain or other medical problems cause insomnia, these underlying problems need to be treated rather than just addressing the sleep symptoms resulting from these problems.

There are non-drug treatments of insomnia that can be more effective than sleeping pill use. One pillar of these treatments is withdrawal from drugs, the most common of which is caffeine, present not only in coffee but in soft drinks, chocolate and many other foods. Maintaining regular sleep times seven days a week can also be helpful. Alcohol can induce sleep, but produces a rebound sleep disruption a few hours after sleep onset. The American Academy of Sleep Medicine is a nonprofit medical organization which accredits and provides contact information for sleep disorder centers in the United States. The treatment of insomnia by cognitive-behavioral therapy and instruction in good sleep hygiene provides the benefits of drug treatment without the risks associated with their use, and with a better long term outcome.

Alcohol and Drug Abuse Can Cause or Mask Sleep Disorders

Regina Patrick

In the following viewpoint Regina Patrick warns that failure to acknowledge drug or alcohol abuse during a sleep study can prevent effective treatment for a sleep disorder. Alcohol and illicit drugs alter the activity of the same neurotransmitters in the brain that control sleep. The chronic use of alcohol leads to reduced amounts of both REM (rapid eye movement) sleep and slow-wave sleep, so recovering alcoholics often have insomnia, and if they use alcohol to get to sleep, that makes it worse. Addictive drugs also adversely affect sleep, yet a preexisting sleep disorder can be a risk factor for addiction. It is important, she says, to reveal any hidden drug use. Patrick is a registered polysomnographic technologist and a contributing writer for *Sleep Review* magazine.

Patients with drug or alcohol addiction may not be willing to report these problems during a sleep study or may not see themselves as having an issue with dependency. Denial or failure to acknowledge drug

SOURCE: Regina Patrick, "Dazed, Confused, and Tired: When Substance Abuse Grips Sleep," *Sleep Review,* March 2009, pp. 23–25. Copyright © Allied Media LLC. Reproduced by permission.

or alcohol abuse can lead to negative health consequences and also can thwart effective treatment for a sleep disorder. However, when sleep professionals develop a keen eye for when illicit drugs are impacting a patient's sleep, they can help accurately treat the patient's sleep disorder. . . .

Alcohol and illicit drug use alter the activity of various neurotransmitters in the brain. Sleep, which depends on the activity of the same neurotransmitters, is affected by alcohol and illicit drug use.

Alcohol's Influence on Sleep

Alcohol (more accurately, ethanol) increases the release of norepinephrine and dopamine and increases the production of beta-endorphin (a neuropeptide that binds with opiate receptors). This initially creates a "high" and sense of well-being. Despite these excitatory effects, alcohol is in actuality a central nervous system depressant. . . .

Chronic alcohol abuse leads to reduced amounts of rapid eye movement (REM) sleep and slow wave sleep, and difficulty in initiating and maintaining sleep. Recovering alcoholics often struggle with insomnia. As a result, they will use alcohol to get to sleep, which in turn can lead to relapse.

Various studies have found that insomnia may be a predictor of relapse in recovering alcoholics. For example, a 2001 University of Michigan study by alcohol addiction researcher Kirk J. Brower et al compared the rate of relapse of alcoholic insomniac subjects with that of alcoholics without insomnia. Both groups had a baseline polysomnographic (PSG) recording and then were followed for 12 weeks. All subjects underwent a second PSG 6 weeks after the study began and a third PSG at 12 weeks. Sleep parameters such as sleep-onset latency, wake after sleep onset, and total sleep time were recorded for each group. Each subject took the self-administered 175-item Sleep Disorder Questionnaire (SDQ), which gives an idea of the subject's perception of their sleep.

They were asked to estimate how long it took to go to sleep, how long they felt they were awake during the night, and how long they had slept. Brower and associates found that the subjects' perception of insomnia was validated by PSG, which showed that the subjects had increased latency to sleep onset, increased amounts of wake after sleep onset, and lower sleep efficiency. Relapse during the first 6 weeks of the 12-week period had a high correlation with subjects who believed they had difficulty maintaining sleep. The researchers later did a follow-up assessment with 43% of the subjects an average of 5 months after they had completed their alcohol treatment program. They noted that relapse after treatment was greater among those subjects who had insomnia at the baseline PSG recording. Brower and associates concluded that questioning alcoholics about insomnia and other sleep problems could potentially prevent relapse and improve recovery.

Impact of Marijuana on Sleep

The leaves of the marijuana plant contain the psychoactive chemical tetrahydrocannabinol (THC). THC binds to cannabinoid receptors in the brain. . . . Cannabinoid activity in these areas results in a sense of pleasure, euphoria, altered time perception, and drowsiness. Withdrawal from marijuana can impair sleep quality due to irritability, restlessness, insomnia, and physical symptoms such as nausea, sweating, and increased body temperature. Heavy marijuana users attempting to quit will resort to using the drug to ameliorate these withdrawal symptoms. This leads to a high relapse rate.

With the hope of improving marijuana abstinence, researchers Margaret Haney et al. investigated using the drug divalproex (trade name Depakote) to lessen the insomnia and negative mood associated with withdrawal. . . . Subjects were all actively using marijuana addicts who smoked about six cigarettes each day for 6 to 7 days each week. They were given a modified St. Mary's Hospital Sleep Questionnaire that asked them to answer questions such as: "I slept well last night," "I woke up early this morning," "I fell asleep easily last night," "I feel clear-headed this morning," "I woke up often last night," and "I am satisfied with my sleep last night." They rated their answer on a scale ranging from "not at all" to "extremely." They were also asked to estimate how many hours they slept the previous night.

The study was a double-blind cross-over study. Subjects, while continuing to smoke marijuana, were initially given either a placebo drug or divalproex for 14 days as an outpatient. The subjects then went into an inpatient setting where they were given divalproex for 15 days and marijuana use could be controlled for three conditions: baseline (days 1 to 4), active marijuana (days 5 to 8), or placebo marijuana (days 9 to 14). (The subjects moved

Alcohol and drug use alter the activity of brain transmitters that control sleep and lead to reduced REM and slow-wave sleep. **(Photo Researchers, Inc.)**

out on day 15.) After completing this, the subjects were crossed over to take either divalproex or the placebo drug for 14 days as an outpatient. They then underwent another 15-day inpatient treatment.

Haney and associates found that when divalproex was taken during the inpatient placebo marijuana days 9 to 14 (ie, withdrawal condition), subjects reported a worsened mood and subjectively believed they had increased problems with sleepiness, difficulty maintaining sleep, and awakening earlier than desired. Objectively, PSG showed that divalproex had actually improved the subjects' total sleep time. Despite this objective improvement, divalproex did not prove useful in enhancing recovery. Haney and associates believe that marijuana addiction recovery involves improving both the objective measures of sleep and the subjective perception of sleep quality.

> **FAST FACT**
>
> Like illegal drugs, prescription drugs and even some over-the-counter drugs may either aggravate sleep disorders or mask them.

Cocaine Takes Its Toll on Sleep

Cocaine is a powdered substance derived from leaves of the coca plant. It blocks the reuptake of dopamine and exerts this effect on . . . the "reward" pathways in the brain. The excess dopaminergic stimulation in these areas results in a burst of euphoria and energy. Chronic cocaine use can lead to problems with insomnia and restlessness.

Recovering cocaine addicts note improved sleep after a period of abstinence, but a group of Yale University School of Medicine researchers headed by Peter T. Morgan recently found that recovering cocaine addicts may actually suffer from hidden insomnia. In a 23-day study, PSG recording of 12 abstinent cocaine addicts revealed that total sleep time and sleep latency were at their worst by days 10 to 14. Continued abstinence to day 23 of the study did not improve sleep, yet the subjects believed their sleep had improved. Morgan and associates concluded that abstinent cocaine addicts, while subjectively feeling better, are unaware of having hidden insomnia. Other researchers have similarly found that sleep quality worsens with continued abstinence and caution that this may increase the risk of relapse in the cocaine addict.

Heroin Harms Healthy Sleep

Heroin is a synthetic substance similar in chemical structure to morphine. It crosses the blood-brain barrier and is converted into morphine in the brain. Heroin binds to opiate receptors located in areas involved in emotion (eg, amygdala) and the reward system (eg, ventral tegmentum). This leads to the euphoria experienced by users. Chronic heroin use results in increased wakefulness, frequent arousals during sleep, decreased total sleep time, and decreased amounts of slow wave sleep and REM sleep with REM sleep being more disrupted than slow wave sleep. Insomnia resulting from opiate abuse can lead to depression, which in turn can result in drug relapse.

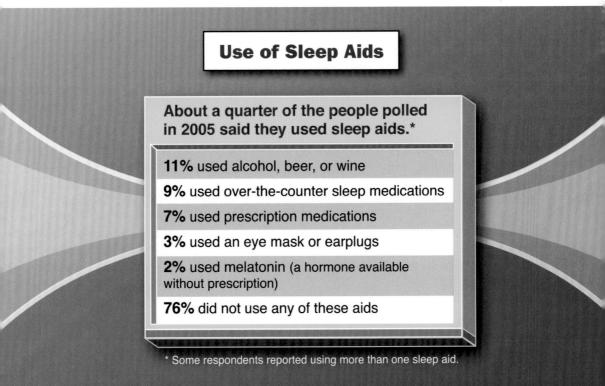

Use of Sleep Aids

About a quarter of the people polled in 2005 said they used sleep aids.*

11% used alcohol, beer, or wine

9% used over-the-counter sleep medications

7% used prescription medications

3% used an eye mask or earplugs

2% used melatonin (a hormone available without prescription)

76% did not use any of these aids

* Some respondents reported using more than one sleep aid.

Taken from: 2005 Sleep in America poll, National Sleep Foundation.

Methamphetamine and MDMA (Ecstasy)

Chronic use of methamphetamine or MDMA can result in insomnia. Chronic MDMA use results in decreased total sleep time and decreased stage 2 sleep. Withdrawal from amphetamine drugs can cause hypersomnia, irritability, and restlessness. These symptoms may lead a person to relapse.

A drug-dependent person may come to a sleep center with complaints of sleep problems such as insomnia or excessive sleepiness, but may not admit to or be aware of the role that alcohol or drug addiction may be playing in their problems and therefore may not mention the drug use. Ironically, a preexisting sleep problem can be a risk factor for addiction since a person may self-medicate in an effort to sleep or remain awake. These factors make improving sleep difficult in someone with suspected drug addiction. However, careful questioning about drug use and sleep symptoms may reveal hidden drug usage and improve treatment efforts for a sleep disorder and drug-addiction recovery.

Narcolepsy Is Often Overlooked in Adolescents

Amber Patterson and Ramalinga Reddy

In the following viewpoint Amber Patterson and Ramalinga Reddy describe the case of a sixteen-year-old patient whose parents said he had passed out after finding it hard to breathe. A sleep study showed that he had narcolepsy, a condition often overlooked in diagnosing teens although it most commonly begins in adolescence. The patient improved with medication but had not yet been allowed to get a driver's license because driving with uncontrolled narcolepsy is dangerous. Reddy is a clinical professor in the division of pediatric pulmonary medicine at the University of Toledo College of Medicine and St. Vincent Mercy Children's Hospital in Ohio. At the time this article was written, Patterson was a third-year resident at the hospital.

A 16-year-old boy presented for evaluation of asthma and exercise-induced bronchospasm. His parents recalled an episode 2 months earlier in which the patient, while jumping on a trampoline and wrestling with his brother, felt like he could not catch his breath. He took a puff of his rescue inhaler, and soon after, passed out. He remained unresponsive for 2 hours.

The teen had been taken to a hospital, where he was extensively evaluated for presumed syncope [fainting] by the pediatric cardiology and pediatric neurology teams. The results of all studies and laboratory tests, including a toxicology screen, ECG [electrocardiogram], echocardiogram, electroencephalogram, and CT [computed tomography] scan of the brain, were within normal limits. After 3 days, he was discharged. No cause of the syncopal episode had been identified. Results of an outpatient Holter monitor [wearable heart monitor] study and a tilt table test [a test for syncope] were normal.

Within the first 3 minutes of the time during which this history was obtained, the patient had fallen asleep. When asked later what he remembered from the episode of 2 months ago, the patient gave a slightly different story. He said he had been listening to a friend tell a joke when he started laughing and passed out. The patient denied use of caffeine, drugs, or cigarettes. He stated that he tires easily in school and that his grades have dropped.

His medical history consisted of mild intermittent asthma, allergies, tympanostomy [procedure to drain the middle ear] with tube placement, and attention deficit hyperactivity disorder [ADHD]. He had had no cardiac problems or seizures. His medications included albuterol as needed and methylphenidate daily. His mother and brother had asthma and allergic disease, and his father had obstructive sleep apnea and narcolepsy. In fact, soon after the patient had fallen asleep, the father also fell asleep.

When examined, the patient appeared comfortable, alert, and cooperative. Height and weight were at the 50th percentile. He had narrow nasal passages with slight

FAST FACT

Researchers from the University of Arkansas–Little Rock found that fewer than 4 percent of pediatricians' patients were diagnosed with a sleep problem, which is far below the rate of children's and teens' sleep problems reported in epidemiological studies.

deviation of the nasal septum. Physical findings were otherwise normal.

Diagnostic Tests

Results of office-based pulmonary function studies and a chest radiograph were normal. To investigate further, overnight polysomnography was performed the next evening followed by a multiple sleep latency test (MSLT). Human leukocyte antigen (HLA) typing for narcolepsy was also ordered. The polysomnogram indicated pathological sleepiness on the basis of the short amount of time that it took for the patient to lapse into rapid eye movement (REM) sleep. The patient had 1 central apnea [pause in breathing] and 9 hypopneas [episodes of abnormally slow breathing]; the apnea/hypopnea index was 1.3 events per hour. This normal apnea/hypopnea

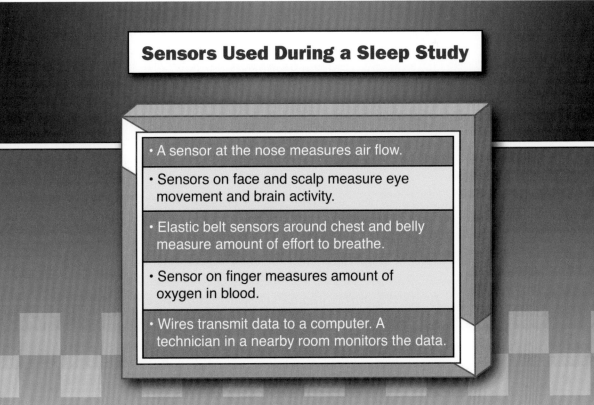

Sensors Used During a Sleep Study

- A sensor at the nose measures air flow.
- Sensors on face and scalp measure eye movement and brain activity.
- Elastic belt sensors around chest and belly measure amount of effort to breathe.
- Sensor on finger measures amount of oxygen in blood.
- Wires transmit data to a computer. A technician in a nearby room monitors the data.

Taken from: National Heart, Lung, and Blood Institute, National Institutes of Health.

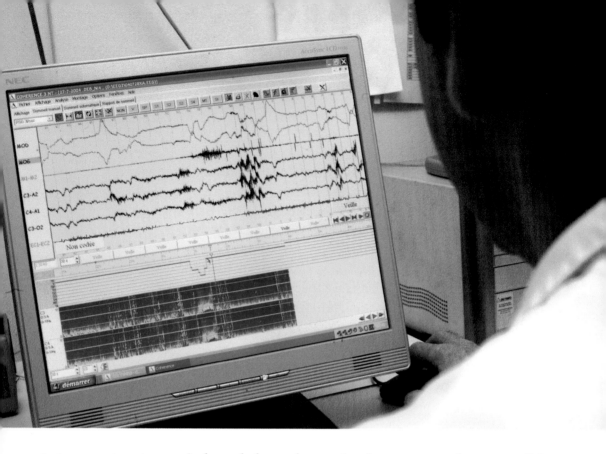

A sleep expert reads the polysomnographic recordings of a sleeping patient. Polysomnography is the study of physiological activity redundant during sleep. (PHANIE/Photo Researchers, Inc.)

index ruled out obstructive sleep apnea as the cause of his excessive daytime sleepiness.

The MSLT showed that in all 4 naps, the patient slept and achieved REM sleep. Mean sleep latency, or the average time it took the patient to fall asleep for all 4 naps, was 52 seconds. These study results, along with the patient's clinical presentation, were diagnostic for narcolepsy, even though the results of HLA typing for narcolepsy were negative.

This patient's initial presentation of "passing out" is similar to what many think of as syncope. However, not all cases of sudden loss of consciousness and postural tone are syncope. It is important to consider all entities in the differential diagnosis of apparent syncope, which could include cardiac, neurological, metabolic, psychiatric, and other causes. . . .

Narcolepsy is often forgotten in adolescents, despite its onset being most common during adolescence; in fact, 90% of persons with narcolepsy have symptoms before age 25 years. Classic findings include frequent (2 to 6) daily, irresistible sleep attacks, after which the patient feels refreshed. The attacks can occur in unusual situations, such as while standing, talking, or even driving. Cataplexy, a sudden loss of muscle tone brought on by intense emotion (eg, laughing) or physical activity, is seen in some patients. Episodes usually last only seconds to minutes, although they have been known to last hours (a phenomenon known as status cataplexicus). We believe this patient was in a state of status cataplexicus during his 2-hour loss of consciousness.

Narcolepsy: An Overview

Diagnosis. Although not a true cause of syncope, narcolepsy remains in the differential diagnosis and must be considered when other life-threatening and common causes of syncope have been ruled out. A phenomenon unique to narcolepsy is sleep-onset REM periods, or SOREMPs. Instead of progressing in a normal sleep pattern from non-REM sleep into REM sleep, persons with narcolepsy can fall directly into REM sleep. This can be documented, as seen in this patient, by overnight polysomnography and MSLT and is diagnostic for narcolepsy.

MSLT is done during the day after an overnight sleep study. The patient is given several opportunities to nap at 2-hour intervals in the hope of quantifying short-latency onset of REM sleep.

Nocturnal polysomnography that excludes other pathological sleep disorders (eg, obstructive sleep apnea) and MSLT that documents a mean sleep latency of less than 8 minutes, in addition to 2 or more SOREMPs, are considered the gold standard for diagnosing narcolepsy. In children, these results in conjunction with a clinical history of excessive daytime sleepiness with or without cataplexy, hypnagogic hallucinations, or sleep paralysis are used to make the diagnosis.

HLA typing and measurement of hypocretin levels in the cerebrospinal fluid are other ways to diagnose narcolepsy; however, negative HLA studies do not exclude the diagnosis. We commonly see patients with a clinical diagnosis of narcolepsy who have negative HLA typing. Although evidence shows a familial predisposition to narcolepsy, there may also be a secondary autoimmune component.

Treatment of narcolepsy consists of a mixture of therapies, including scheduled naps, stimulant medications, and tricyclic antidepressants. . . . Narcolepsy is a serious lifelong condition.

This disorder, which commonly begins in adolescence, can be psychosocially traumatic for a young person. More important, a patient's participation in common activities, such as swimming, cooking, and driving, can be dangerous. Several studies of motor vehicle crash data by age have shown that young people aged 16 to 29 years were most likely to be in crashes caused by the driver falling asleep. Falling asleep while driving could be fatal to the patient and others, and for this reason, it is imperative that a physician discuss driving privileges with any patient with narcolepsy. The AMA [American Medical Association] and National Highway Traffic Safety Administration recommend ceasing or denying driving privileges in those in whom narcolepsy is diagnosed. These privileges may be reinstated once the patient has undergone treatment and no longer has excessive daytime sleepiness or cataplexy. The Epworth Sleepiness Scale can be a useful tool in assessing levels of daytime drowsiness.

Outcome of the Case

On follow-up evaluation, narcolepsy and cataplexy were diagnosed. . . . The patient has noticed gradual improvement in his symptoms of daytime wakefulness but continues to have intermittent sleep attacks, which we feel may be related to poor adherence to his medication regimen. To his dismay, we have not yet permitted him to obtain his driver's license.

Night Terrors Are a Sleep Disorder and Not Just Nightmares

David W. Richards

In the following viewpoint David W. Richards, who has the disorder called night terrors or sleep terrors, explains that this disorder is a sleep disorder and not a psychological problem or possession by demons. Most researchers believe that night terrors are caused by a chemical trigger in the brain, he says, but people who have them are often misdiagnosed as just having nightmares. Night terrors are not the same as nightmares, which occur in the dreaming stage of sleep. Night terrors occur prior to that stage of sleep. Richards describes what night terrors are like and some of the things that may trigger them. Richards works as the director of information technologies for a large town in Connecticut. In his free time he operates a website for people with night terrors, the Night Terrors Resource Center.

A fter spending the last 20+ years of my life experiencing Night Terrors, I decided to find out more about this sleep disorder. I hope the following will help shed some light on the subject. The first

SOURCE: David W. Richards, "Night Terrors Homepage" and "Night Terrors Additional Information," www.nightterrors.org, 2006. Reproduced by permission.

How Sleep Stages Differ

Stage	Bodily Activity	Depth of Sleep	Thought process	Miscellaneous
0 Awake	Slows down; decreased muscle tension.	Borderline wakefulness	Relaxation; mind wanders; awareness dulls.	Heart rate, pulse, temperature, and blood pressure slightly diminished.
1	Eyes roll slowly on falling asleep; eyes quiescent in later stage 1 periods. Body movements slowed.	Light sleep; easily awakened; might deny being asleep if awakened.	Drifting thoughts and floating sensation.	Temperature, heart rate, pulse decline. Regular breathing. May have hypnagogic hallucinations on falling asleep.
2	Eyes quiet. Few body movements. Snoring is common.	Light to moderate sleep. Relatively easy to awaken. Eyes will not see if open.	Some thought fragments; memory processes diminished; may describe vague dream if awakened.	Decreased heart rate, pulse, blood pressure, temperature, and metabolic rate; regular breathing with increased airway resistance.
3	Occasional movement; eyes quiescent.	Deep sleep; takes louder sounds to be awakened.	Rarely able to remember thoughts. A few vaguely formed dreams. Possible memory consolidation.	Metabolic rate, pulse, heart rate, blood pressure, and temperature decrease further. Increased secretion of growth hormones.
4	Occasional movement; eyes quiet.	Deepest sleep; very difficult to awaken.	Virtually oblivious; very poor recall of thoughts if awakened; possibly involved in memory consolidation.	Continued decline in heart rate, temperature, and metabolic rates. Increased secretion of growth hormone (possibly to restore bodily tissues).
REM	Large muscles paralyzed. Fingers, toes, and facial muscles twitch. Erections, snoring uncommon.	Variable. If sound is incorporated into dream, then harder to awake.	80 percent dreaming; good vivid dream recall, especially later in the evening. Possibly involved in unconscious conflict resolution.	Heart rate 5 percent greater than above stages. Pulse, temperature, and metabolic rate increase. Irregular breathing; one-half extra breath per minute.

thing I found was that this problem goes by a few different names. Sleep Terrors, Sleep Terror Disorder, Night Terrors, Pavor Nocturnus and then the mouthful DSM-IV AXIS I: 307.46 are just a few. This fact made it very difficult to do an internet search for more information. Another problem I ran into was that HSP (hallucinatory sleep disorder) has some similarities to Night Terrors. . . .

[My aim] is to help people understand that there are medical solutions and reasons for Night Terrors. You will not be preached to here or told that Satan caused your Night Terrors. Night Terrors are a medical ailment and not demon possession. . . .

Sleep labs across the United States and Canada have shown through sleep studies, that Night Terrors happen due to increased brain activity.

The common thought among researchers is that a chemical trigger in the brain causes your brain to "misfire" and cause a Night Terror. These misfires can be caused by many factors such as stress and various other medical ailments.

People who have night terrors are often misdiagnosed. The most common [misdiagnosis] is [that the person had] a simple nightmare. Any of you who have had a Night Terror can say they aren't even close! Another common misdiagnosis (especially among veterans) is PTSD, or Post Traumatic Stress Disorder. For this reason I have included a description of the difference between nightmares and night terrors.

Night Terrors symptoms [include] sudden awakening from sleep, persistent fear or terror that occurs at night, screaming, sweating, confusion, rapid heart rate, inability to explain what happened, usually no recall of "bad dreams" or nightmares, [maybe] a vague sense of frightening images. Many people see spiders, snakes, animals or people in the room, are unable to fully awake, [are] difficult to comfort, with no memory of the event on awakening the next day.

Night Terror or Nightmare?

Nightmares occur during the dream phase of sleep known as REM [rapid eye movement] sleep. Most people enter the REM stage of sleep sometime after 90 minutes of sleep. The circumstances of the nightmare will frighten the sleeper, who usually will wake up with a vivid memory of a long movie-like dream. Night Terrors, on the other hand, occur during a phase of deep non-REM sleep usually within an hour after the subject goes to bed. This is also known as stage 4 [sleep]. During a Night Terror, which may last anywhere from five to twenty minutes, the person is still asleep, although the sleeper's eyes may be open. When the subject does wake up, they usually have no recollection of the episode other than a sense of fear. This, however, is not always the case. Quite a few people interviewed can remember portions of the Night Terror, and some remember the whole thing.

Although Night Terrors can occur anytime in a person's life span, [they are] most commonly reported in children between the ages of three and five. (However, more recent studies have turned up showing that many adults as well as children as young as six months experience Night Terrors on a weekly basis.) Night Terrors usually occur fifteen minutes to one hour after going to sleep. I personally experience mine at just about the 45 minute mark. The longer the person is in NREM [non-REM] (the stages before REM) before the Night Terror strikes, the more petrified they will be when it occurs. Keep in mind though not everyone falls to sleep in the same amount of time as others. This makes a sleep study about the only way of determining what stage of sleep you are in when these events occur.

Night Terrors have been shown to appear in stage 4 of sleep. This is just one thing that separates them from nightmares which can occur anytime in sleep. It is possible to make a Night Terror occur in some people, simply by touching or awakening them during stage

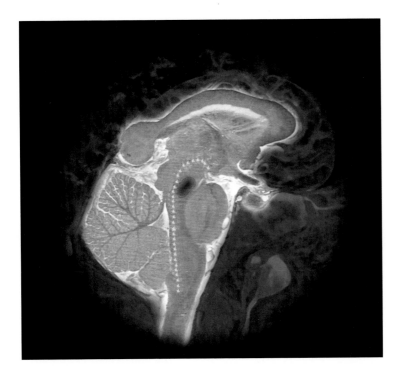

A sagittal (from above) view of the human brain shows the areas related to sleeping and dreaming. Slow-wave sleep is colored pink; the area of non-REM sleep, where night terrors occur, is colored yellow; and the REM sleep area (dreaming) is colored green. **(James Cavallini/ Photo Researchers, Inc.)**

4 of sleep. Why Night Terrors occur is still a mystery. The mind is supposed to be practically void during the deeper stages of sleep. Most sufferers will awake gasping, moaning, crying—but more often screaming.

Breathing rapidly they will sit up in bed with a wide-eyed, terror-filled stare. This panic will often last anywhere from five to twenty minutes. I find the most amazing aspect of Night Terrors is that it generates a heart rate of 160 to 170 beats per minute. This is much faster than the normal heart rate that can be attained under most stressful circumstances.

Triggers for Night Terrors

Some things that can help bring out a Night Terror are stress, medications that affect the brain, . . . being over-tired or eating a heavy meal before going to bed. Combining all of the above I can usually guarantee an occurrence for myself. Many different medical ailments contribute to the frequency of Night Terrors. The listed items *do not* cause Night Terrors, they just seem to put your body into the state where a Night Terror can manifest itself. People without Night Terrors will not have a Night Terror just by trying the above.

There seems to be a common thread in how Night Terrors manifest themselves. Many people who remember the Night Terror have talked about seeing animals or people. Most people describe the person that they see as dark and shadowy and feel that the person is going to hurt them. Quite a few people see snakes and spiders. At first I thought people were seeing only things they are afraid of during waking hours. After more research I found that only a small percentage of people were afraid of what they see (in Night Terrors) during waking hours.

Some people remember the Night Terror. Some don't. There is no explanation [as] to why some have no recall of the events during a Night Terror. If you are told by a doctor that the fact you remember your Night Terror [means] it must not be a Night Terror, find another doctor.

Many people have written me to disagree, but I have found the best method of controlling someone during a Night Terror is to hug and reassure them and tell them that everything is all right. Agree with what they are saying and doing. Sometimes it is not possible to hug them. Don't try to force physical contact. *Do not* yell at them or tell them they are only dreaming as this seems to only upset them even more. Move objects that can injure the person out of the way. This method seems to work better in children rather than in adults. (Adults are a little more physical.) The most important thing to remember is that someone having a Night Terror does not know what they are doing. Make sure that there is not

FAST FACT

In 1953 scientists found that a person's closed eyes move rapidly when he or she is dreaming, which led to the discovery that sleep has distinct stages of brain functioning.

anything nearby that they can hurt themselves or others with. It is perfectly safe to wake someone who is having a Night Terror. Please be gentle!

It is also interesting to note that two other disorders, sleepwalking and bed wetting, are experienced during stage 4 of sleep. Even more interesting is the fact that all three of these sleep disorders often run in families. My father only realized he had Night Terrors after I started researching the subject. Some families will dismiss Night Terrors as nightmares and grow more and more upset, blaming the problem on television or other before-bed stimuli. Episodic Night terrors *do not* signify psychological problems. Don't ever tell the subject that nothing has happened. It is OK to tell that person, the next morning, they had a Night Terror. It is, however, not advisable to notify children the next morning if they do not remember.

Sleep Paralysis Is Normal

Rebecca Turner

In the following viewpoint Rebecca Turner explains what sleep paralysis is and why it happens. It is the naturally occurring state that keeps people from acting out their dreams, she says, and is not dangerous. It is usually switched off upon awakening, but some people become aware that their muscles are paralyzed when falling asleep or waking up, which is frightening and may lead to panic. It can be accompanied by a so-called hypnagogic hallucination of a menacing presence in the room, often one that tries to harm the sufferer. Turner lists ways to quickly stop an episode of sleep paralysis, but, in her opinion, the best way to deal with hypnagogic hallucinations is to transform them into positive visionary experiences or lucid dreams. Turner is a writer and website designer who has much personal experience in lucid dreaming. She lives in New Zealand.

SOURCE: Rebecca Turner, "How to Stop Sleep Paralysis and Have Lucid Dreams," www.world-of-lucid-dreaming.com, 2010. Reproduced by permission.

Sleep paralysis [SP] is a naturally occurring state that begins when we fall asleep each night. It arises before REM [rapid eye movement, or dreaming] sleep to stop us from acting out our dreams. This is vital to keep us out of harm's way when we are unconscious—and if we want a good night's sleep. It is a basic protection mechanism.

You normally don't notice the paralysis happening because you are asleep. Your mind is either totally unconscious—or focused on a dream. And when you wake up, the paralysis is switched off in time with your conscious awakening.

However, some people become aware of sleep paralysis, feeling their muscles are partially or totally paralyzed. This feeling can be accompanied by terrifying hypnagogic hallucinations, usually of a menacing stranger.

If you are a sufferer, fear not. Dream research has revealed reliable ways for you to immediately stop sleep paralysis in its tracks, or to use this borderland state of consciousness as a gateway to vivid lucid dreams and out of body experiences.

SP is not physically dangerous. It is a natural protection mechanism. It is far better to wake up temporarily paralyzed than to be running around in your sleep. When people suffer from isolated Sleep Paralysis (iSP), they become conscious of their own inability to move. This can be scary and cause them to panic and fight the paralysis, which only leads to further struggling and greater fear. In extreme cases where SP lasts for 10 minutes or more, the sufferer may ache the next day from straining to break free from the muscle paralysis.

> **FAST FACT**
>
> In the past, sleep paralysis accompanied by hallucinations was sometimes misdiagnosed as mental illness.

Hypnagogic Hallucinations

If fear takes grip during an episode, the sleep paralysis can be accompanied by a sense of menace or a dark presence in

Artist Henri Fuseli's *The Nightmare* shows an incubus sitting on a sleeping woman's chest. Sleep paralysis victims often experience difficulty in breathing and feelings of strangulation. **(Founders Society purchase with Mr. and Mrs. Bert L. Smokler and Mr. and Mrs. Lawremce A. Fleischman funds. Bridgeman Art Library)**

the room. There are many explanations for this, although no-one really knows what the dominant trigger is. It may be a combination of our evolutionary fears of being hunted and perceiving benign sounds or movement as a threat, plus our innate ability to see human faces just about anywhere: in the wood grain of a door, or a dark shadow in the night.

Either way, the half-dreaming brain *sees* what it wants to see, even if it means conjuring up a hellish vision of a demon coming into the room.

This has been documented around the world for hundreds of years, in various forms. Consider the famous painting by Henri Fuseli of an incubus attacking a sleeping woman, in *The Nightmare*.

Often in cases of iSP, the nightmare figure approaches the bed and tries to harm the sufferer, by strangling or molesting them, or sitting on their chest. The experience can be heightened by memories of sexual abuse or Post Traumatic Stress Disorder (PTSD). This also explains stories of alien abductions which share all the same features.

The Causes of Sleep Paralysis

Scientists know very little about the causes of this sleep disorder. As far as the paralysis mechanism goes, there is a theory that motor neurons in the brain are inhibited—which means the signals to move the body don't get through to the spine as they should. This leaves your limbs feeling waxy and unresponsive.

It's common enough that 40% of the world's population may experience this condition at least once in our lives. Some people report it regularly, in which case it is regarded as a sleep disorder (iSP). You may be more prone to it if you:

• Suffer from narcolepsy
• Suffer sleep deprivation
• Are under a lot of stress
• Suffer other sleep disorders
• Have frequent naps

How to Stop Sleep Paralysis

Here are some practical tips for helping to quickly dissipate an episode of SP:

• Relax your body into the paralysis—*don't* fight it
• Think peaceful, relaxing thoughts; pray or sing in your mind
• Wiggle your fingers and toes if you can
• Move your eyes and look around the room
• Focus on breathing deeply and moving your mouth

Age of First Sleep Paralysis Episode

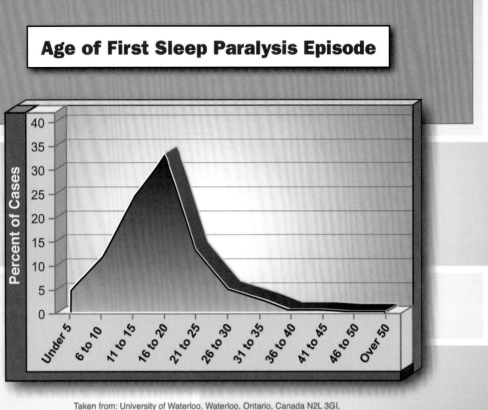

Taken from: University of Waterloo, Waterloo, Ontario, Canada N2L 3GI, http://watarts.uwaterloo.ca/~acheyne/spdoc/Techreport.pdf.

Once your brain realizes that parts of your body are still awake, it will shut off the paralysis mechanism and you will return to full wakefulness.

However, if you start to experience hypnagogic hallucinations, you will need to take the more advanced approaches described in . . . [books] on reliably transforming SP with hallucinations into positive visionary experiences and lucid dreams [dreams that are consciously directed].

Believe it or not, lucid dreamers attempt to induce sleep paralysis on purpose. When you enter SP deliberately, it is with a specific goal in mind. You are focused on your own internal visualizations and you know that the paralysis is a sign that it's working. So you don't react with the same fear as the unsuspecting victim who wakes up paralyzed in the middle of the night.

Without this fear, sleep paralysis can be the gateway to visionary states of being. You can experience out of body travel (whatever your spiritual beliefs) or vivid lucid dreams and inner journeys. Indeed, the father of lucid dream research, Dr Stephen LaBerge of Stanford University, once said: "[Sleep paralysis] . . . is not only nothing to be frightened of, it can be something to be sought after and cultivated. . . . Just step over and you're in the world of lucid dreams."

The Public and Physicians Alike Are Uninformed About the Dangers of Adult Sleepwalking

Shelley R. Gunn and W. Stewart Gunn

In the following viewpoint Shelley R. Gunn tells about the serious injury her son suffered while sleepwalking during a trip and points out that the dangers of sleepwalking in adults are not well known to the public. She describes things sleepwalkers have done, explains the physical causes of sleepwalking, and lists precautions that should be taken when a person is known to be prone to sleepwalking. Gunn is a clinical pathologist at the START Center for Cancer Care in San Antonio, Texas, and a clinical assistant professor at the University of Texas Health Science Center. W. Stewart Gunn is her son.

Sleepwalking generally occurs in the dark and has remained there, both literally and figuratively, for centuries. The image that comes most readily to mind is a cartoon person, amiably and aimlessly wandering the hallway, with arms outstretched and eyes closed. But sleepwalking is not funny; it is a sleep disorder known to specialists as somnambulism. Many adult sleepwalkers, with eyes open, perform purposeful acts such as eating half a bag of chips and putting the rest in the microwave, taking all their shoes from the closet and lining them [up] on the windowsill, rearranging furniture, or climbing out a window in the middle of the night—activities that are essentially benign when a person is conscious but that, when they occur during somnambulism, are potentially dangerous to the sleepwalker or other people. More frighteningly, increasing numbers of so-called "sleepdriving" cases are being reported in which somnambulists get in their cars and drive sometimes long distances, disregarding lanes, stoplights, and stationary objects, and, after waking up, having no memory of what they did.

An Increase in Sleepwalking

Although these nocturnal wanderings may seem extremely odd to nonsleepwalkers, such mechanistic and automatic activities are part of the spectrum of behavior associated with somnambulism, which is estimated to affect close to 2 percent of the adult population worldwide. Sleepwalking and other sleep disorders appear to be on the rise in our demanding and fast-paced society, in which getting a good night's sleep seems to be increasingly difficult. Many people resort to prescription (or nonprescription) drugs to induce sleep, but sometimes this only compounds the problem. Sleep deprivation, especially in combination with drugs and alcohol, is known to induce sleepwalking in some people, and behavior while sleepwalking is extremely unpredictable, particularly in a new environment. Any adult with a tendency to sleepwalk has the potential to experience an accident and can be at risk of real injury. But, until recently, published reports of injuries as a result of sleepwalking were rare, and somnambulism and other sleep disorders are frequently overlooked in the medical school curriculum.

Although I am a teacher of medical neuroscience, the dangers of sleepwalking would probably never have come to my attention had my son Stewart (who joins me in writing this article) not sleepwalked out a second-story window into an alley, sustaining serious injuries, on the night he arrived for a British Studies program at St. John's College in Oxford, England. His potentially fatal experience with sleepwalking demanded a reexamination of this overlooked topic and raised many questions during his convalescence. Had other people been seriously injured while sleepwalking? If so, were these random and rare events, or had we encountered the tip of an unexplored iceberg?

An Uninformed Public and Medical Community

By searching the medical literature and interviewing other sleepwalkers, we found that sleepwalking accidents and injuries, more common than usually believed, are a definite health hazard for both the sleepwalker and other people. But such accidents are not well known, because both the general public and physicians are uninformed about somnambulism.

In this article, we explore current theories about both the causes and the management of adult sleepwalking, while seeking to increase awareness of its hidden dangers. Sleep medicine needs to be an integral part of the medical school curriculum, and physicians as well as the general public should be aware that, unlike sleepwalking in children, somnambulism in adults is a potentially dangerous disorder. Both treatment of the disorder—when possible—and prevention of accidents are of paramount importance for the sleepwalker and for unsuspecting people who may find themselves in the sleepwalker's path.

Stewart's Experience of Sleepwalking

Stewart arrived in Oxford, sleep-deprived after the long trip from Texas, and checked into his second-floor dormitory at St. John's College on a warm July day. The wide open windows had no screens and were surrounded by scaffolding. Even though he had been awake for more than 30 hours, he chose to postpone sleep until after dinner in order to adjust to British time. He fell asleep easily, but, when he awoke about 2:00 a.m., he was lying face down on a cobblestone street that he did not recognize. He had absolutely no recall of having left his dorm room, walking through several doorways, and stepping out a window onto the scaffolding from which he must have fallen into the alley. After unsuccessfully trying to lift himself off the cobblestone street, he dragged himself toward what appeared to be a road and was discovered by the British police. He had fractured his spine and right wrist in the accident, but thankfully had no permanent neurological damage.

> **FAST FACT**
>
> Sleep eating is a relatively rare variation of sleepwalking that is listed as a separate sleep disorder. Sleep eaters are unaware of their behavior and may eat large quantities of food and sometimes even nonfood items.

At the same time that Stewart was recovering at the John Radcliffe Hospital, *CNN News* reported the story of a London teenaged girl who was rescued from the top of a crane, which she had climbed while sleepwalking and then gone back to sleep on the support beam—fortunately catching the attention of a pedestrian who notified the police. The hospital staff caring for Stewart found this amusing and suggested that the two young sleepwalkers get to know each other. Although Stewart and the girl never met, their similar stories motivated us to start looking further into the prevalence and possible causes of adult sleepwalking.

Experiences of Sleepwalkers

We did not have to look far for stories. The paramedic who helped take Stewart to Gatwick Airport had an adult sister who had injured herself while sleepwalking, and we encountered a woman on the flight home whose son had repeatedly sleepwalked onto a balcony. An acquaintance

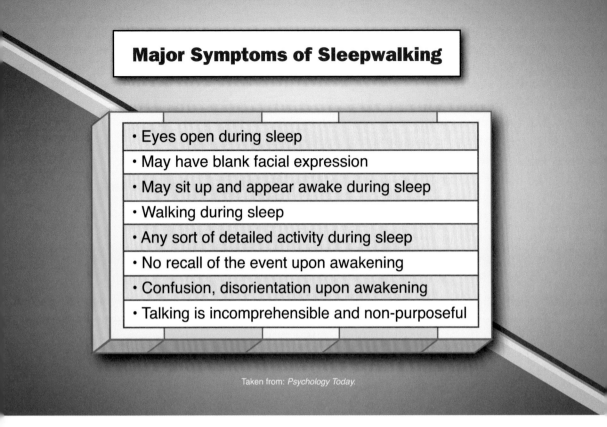

Major Symptoms of Sleepwalking

- Eyes open during sleep
- May have blank facial expression
- May sit up and appear awake during sleep
- Walking during sleep
- Any sort of detailed activity during sleep
- No recall of the event upon awakening
- Confusion, disorientation upon awakening
- Talking is incomprehensible and non-purposeful

Taken from: *Psychology Today.*

called to relate how her son not only regularly disassembled bedside lamps while sleepwalking but was recently found, in his pajamas, pumping gas after sleepdriving to the gas station. In 2003, several cases involving mysterious nighttime accidents, some of which were fatal and initially ruled as suicide, were reported in the *Journal of Forensic Science* by Mark Mahawald, M.D., director of the Minnesota Regional Sleep Disorders Center. These deaths, referred to as "parasomnia pseudo-suicides," were later attributed to complex motor behaviors that can take place during sleepwalking, such as running, climbing, or jumping. One involved a 21-year-old college student who was hit by a semitrailer truck after he ran onto a highway at 4:30 a.m., clad only in his boxer shorts. He had no history of drug abuse or depression, but he and several family members had a history of frequent, complex sleepwalking. A formal review of his case requested by his family resulted in a recommendation by the medical examiner that the cause of death be changed from "suicide" to "accidental death due to sleepwalking."

Other cases described by Mahawald involved falls from balconies, defenestration (jumping from windows), and self-inflicted gunshot wounds by people with a past history of complex sleepwalking behavior and no history of depression. Distinguishing between accidental death and suicide has profound religious, societal, and insurance implications, of course, and many of the families of these victims requested that these pseudo-suicides be re-evaluated as accidental death as a result of a sleep disorder. Some cases of homicidal behavior during sleepwalking have also been reported. The legal defense in these cases has usually been to claim that the action was a "non-insane automatism," meaning that the brain's motor system was fully aroused but consciousness was clouded. In all of these types of cases, a correct diagnosis or verdict can be made only if the family, police, and medical examiners are willing to consider alternative scenarios.

Prescription Drugs as a Risk Factor

Early in 2006, a surge of news reports described complex sleepwalking behaviors that involved binge eating, violent outbursts, and sleepdriving in people who took the medication Ambien (zolpidem).

Ambien, the best-selling prescription sleeping pill in the United States, is a popular alternative to the more traditional benzodiazepines because of its general lack of serious side effects. Since it was introduced in the early 1990s, mild side effects such as nausea, dizziness, and nightmares have been reported in people taking the drug as prescribed. But in 1994 and 1995, the first two cases of sleepwalking attributed to Ambien appeared in the medical literature, followed by an additional six cases during the next 10 years. . . .

A [2006] article in the *New York Times* reported that Ambien is one of the top 10 drugs identified in the blood of impaired drivers, and, in Wisconsin alone, Ambien was identified in 187 drivers arrested from 1999 to 2004. . . .

During the past 10 years, a handful of case reports were published that describe sleepdriving in non-Ambien users. These reports described behavior not unlike that seen in Ambien sleepwalkers: long-distance driving and bizarre behavior, followed by complete amnesia for the event. The unifying question that needs to be addressed is: What is happening in the brain to cause such a disassociation between being awake and being asleep?

Inside the Sleepwalking Brain

In sleepwalkers, however, the states of being awake and being asleep are not mutually exclusive; instead, they occur simultaneously. Parts of the brain are aroused, the eyes are open, and postural muscles are tensed and active, while clear, lucid consciousness remains suspended. Sleepwalkers, who are awake and asleep at the same time, have been described for centuries. Think of Shakespeare's Lady Macbeth: "You see, her eyes are open . . . but their sense is shut."

More analytical descriptions of human sleep became possible at the beginning of the 20th century, with the development of the electroencephalogram (EEG), a device that measures and records the electrical activity of the brain by using flat metal discs [electrodes] placed on the surface of the head. The electrodes are connected by wires to an amplifier and recording machine that convert the electrical signals from the brain into pen-and-paper tracings that resemble waves. Further technological advances have increased the ability of researchers and physicians to analyze sleep and its disorders by using all-night monitoring of not only the brain but also eye and leg movements, respiration, and heart rate through a comprehensive diagnostic test known as polysomnography, conducted in a sleep laboratory.

On the basis of EEG wave patterns, sleep can be broadly divided into rapid eye movement (REM) and non-rapid eye movement (nREM). REM sleep is associated with dreaming and with high-frequency, low-voltage brain waves, whereas nREM sleep is characterized by low-frequency, high-amplitude waves known as slow-wave sleep (SWS). NREM sleep is further divided into stages I to IV, with stages III and IV representing the deepest sleep. A normal sleeping adult will repeatedly alternate between nREM sleep and REM sleep, with each total cycle lasting on average about 90 minutes, and SWS dominating the first third of the night. A person who sleeps for eight hours will progress through four or five cycles during one night's sleep, with REM episodes becoming longer during the course of the night.

During REM sleep, a complete and dramatic loss of muscle tone occurs. This loss is protective, because it prevents the sleeper from acting out dreams. However, sleepwalking generally occurs during stages III and IV, possibly as a result of an incomplete transition from SWS back into REM sleep, and dreams are not commonly associated with these nREM stages. What, therefore, causes sleepwalkers to leave their beds and wander into the night?

Finding the answer to this question has been the goal of much research. . . .

NREM Sleep Instability

Sleep researchers have found that sleepwalking occurs against a background of nREM sleep instability characterized by a particular kind of high-voltage brain wave called hypersynchronous slow delta (HSD). These HSD waves were first described in a May 1965 article in the journal *Science* describing a University of California, Los Angeles (UCLA), study of a group of sleepwalkers who underwent all-night EEG recording using special techniques that allowed them to get up and move around.

HSD waves were recorded both before and during sleep-walking episodes in the UCLA study, and subsequent studies have consistently identified HSD waves associated with sleepwalking. However, the significance and specificity of these waves for sleepwalking have been questioned in subsequent research, because HSD waves have also been identified in the EEGs of people with other sleep disorders, as well as in normal sleep.

According to Christian Guilleminault, M.D., Ph.D., of the Stanford University Sleep Disorders Clinic, HSD waves can be seen normally in the nightly cyclical passage from stable to unstable sleep as the billions of neurons in the human brain are recruited during early stages of nREM sleep into the orderly SWS rhythms of stages III and IV. However, when the HSD wave pattern persists throughout stages III and IV, it is indicative of an interruption in the normal progression of nREM sleep. This disturbance can be interpreted by sleep researchers using a technique called cyclic alternating pattern (CAP) analysis.

CAP analysis is particularly valuable in evaluating nREM disorders of arousal, because these disorders are not generally accompanied by significant changes in the brain processes that can be detected by all-night sleep monitoring using EEG and the other tools of polysomnography. CAP provides a measure of the microstructure of brain waves in sleep instability through analysis of sequences of EEG patterns. If the CAP rate is indicative of abnormal sleep, then it is imperative to search for the instability's cause, which is generally a subtle associated sleep disorder. In a January 2006 article in the journal *Sleep Medicine,* Guilleminault stated that he did not find a "pure" sleepwalker in the most recent 100 cases he studied and that the identification of the underlying cause of sleep instability often led to treatment and elimination of sleepwalking in his patients.

What Happens During Sleepwalking

In chronic sleepwalkers, respiratory syndromes are the most frequently diagnosed accompanying disorders. As a result of the close relation between abnormal retention of carbon dioxide in the blood (a condition known as hypercapnia) and activation of neurons within the brain stem that control sleep and waking, an inability to breathe normally affects neural control of the progression through sleep. Specific respiratory syndromes, including upper airway resistance syndrome, mild obstructive sleep apnea, and sleep-disordered breathing, have been diagnosed as underlying causes of sleep instability. Through CAP analysis of chronic sleepwalkers, researchers have learned that the basic nREM instability accompanying the breathing disorder is present even on nights when no sleepwalking occurs. But the instability almost always completely vanishes when the respiratory problem is successfully treated, usually through the delivery of air to the upper respiratory tract through a specially designed mask (continuous positive airway pressure, or CPAP), or through surgery. . . .

The Stanford University study of chronic sleepwalkers reported by Guilleminault found that sleepwalking was much more likely to be eradicated in patients with treatable respiratory disorders, so it is important to seek an underlying cause of sleep instability for chronic sleepwalkers. The rare cases of "pure" sleepwalking, which appear to have no associated disorder, may represent a subgroup of sleepwalkers in whom nREM sleep instability is the result of genetic factors. Benzodiazepines, the most commonly prescribed drugs for sleepwalking, are only partially effective in eliminating sleepwalking in these patients, so attention must be focused on maintaining a safe sleeping environment to prevent accidents.

Living Safely with Adult Somnambulism

When sleepwalking behavior persists or reemerges in adulthood, it is no longer a relatively benign disorder of childhood, even though the same underlying nREM sleep instability is present at all ages. Occasional injuries have been reported in childhood sleepwalkers, but by the time a child is about 12 years old, when the central nervous system matures, episodes usually disappear—before most children are able to drive or have access to alcohol and guns. The most common automatic, unconscious behavior in young children who sleepwalk is to seek their parents, which is what Stewart did during his childhood sleepwalking episodes.

For adults in whom sleepwalking has become chronic or dangerous, it is thus imperative to address both issues of safety and the eventual elimination of the behavior. Since repeated episodes of somnambulism indicate an underlying nREM sleep instability, physicians must try to identify any associated sleep disorder that could be causing abnormal progression through the stages of sleep. But even if, as is most often the case, a sleep-related breathing disorder is identified, treatment such as CPAP or surgery is not instantly successful, and the inherent dangers of sleepwalking will persist until the cause of nREM instability is completely eliminated. Therefore, safety remains of paramount importance in managing chronic sleepwalking even after diagnosing and starting to treat the underlying disorder. In some sleepwalkers, no treatable cause will be found; for them attention to sleep practices and safeguarding the environment are lifetime challenges.

The real key to sleepwalking safety is knowledge, knowledge of whether a person is a sleepwalker and awareness of the conditions or drugs that increase the possibility of a sleepwalking incident. All prescription sleep medications should be taken exactly as directed. Ambien may not be a good choice for someone with a

history of sleepwalking. If taken with alcohol, Ambien has the potential to induce sleepwalking even in people with no previous history of the disorder. . . .

Avoid Sleep Deprivation

Sleep deprivation is also known to trigger sleepwalking in susceptible persons, possibly as a result of the extremely deep nREM sleep, known as rebound or recovery, sleep, that often occurs after long periods without sleep. Stewart had been awake for more than 35 hours when he finally fell asleep in his Oxford dormitory room, an amount of sleep deprivation that sleep laboratory studies have shown is sufficient to increase the frequency and complexity of somnambulistic episodes during recovery sleep. In some laboratories, artificially inducing sleepwalking by sleep deprivation has been used as a tool in the diagnosis of somnambulism. Known sleepwalkers should therefore do everything possible not to become

Nocturnal wanderings, eating while asleep, and other odd sleep behaviors are all symptoms of somnambulism, which affects 2 percent of the population worldwide. (allOver Photography/Alamy)

sleep deprived, particularly when they cross time zones and sleep the first night in a new environment—all factors in Stewart's Oxford accident. In addition, neither alcohol nor sleep drugs such as Ambien should be taken under these conditions.

Both at home and when traveling, safeguarding the environment should be a top priority for sleepwalkers. Appropriate precautions include choosing lower bunks and ground-floor rooms and bolting shut doors and windows, possibly with a chair placed in front of them (after first locating and not blocking the fire exits.) Beds should be pushed to the wall, and a sleeping partner should sleep on the outside, so the sleepwalker would have to climb over the partner to get out of bed and wander into the night. If possible, bedroom and outer doors should be equipped with alarms and buzzers that are loud enough to awaken the sleepwalker or the family, particularly when traveling by boat because of the risk of falling overboard. Power tools or guns should be stored in locked cabinets with combinations or key entry not amenable to being unlocked in an unconscious state. A sleepwalker should never he allowed to drive while somnambulant, and car keys as well as the car should be made inaccessible at night if there is any tendency to sleepdrive. Contrary to what most people think, it is not dangerous to awaken a sleepwalker, and he or she will probably thank you the next morning upon waking up safely in bed.

"Merry Wanderers of the Night"

For the most part, sleepwalkers have earned their amiable reputation as, in the words of Shakespeare, just "merry wanderers of the night." Whether conducting imaginary orchestras, climbing trees, or taking walks outside clad only in pajamas, they give us a glimpse of the incredible intricacy and complexity of a human brain that is capable of being awake and asleep at the same time. That most people successfully make the journey through the many stages of sleep several times each night is a testimony to the ability of billions of neurons to synchronize themselves into the fundamental biological process required by all organisms—the need to rest. In somnambulism this process has somehow been subverted, but, with a growing public awareness about the hidden dangers of sleepwalking and increasing coverage of sleep medicine in neuroscience textbooks and medical school curricula, we hope that the world is becoming a safer place for all night-time wanderers.

Researchers Are Investigating Crimes Committed While Sleepwalking

Lindsay Lyon

Some people who have apparently committed suicide or acts of violence, including murder, have actually been sleepwalking and are acquitted if this is proved in court. In the following article Lindsay Lyon describes the new field of sleep forensics, to which lawyers and law enforcement officials turn when investigating crimes that are thought to be explained by a sleep problem. The primary aim of specialists in sleep forensics is to do scientific research on sleep disorders, collecting data that may later reveal patterns that shed light on what underlies bizarre sleep behavior. Some of the cases they see, however, turn out to be fake claims, and even true sleepwalkers sometimes commit crimes consciously. Lyon is a reporter for *U.S. News & World Report*.

How the body got there was a mystery. More than 12 hours earlier, the man had emerged from successful back surgery. Now, clad only in underwear, he was outside, dead, wedged between a generator and a wall. He was six floors below the hospital roof-top. Had he jumped to his death? Had he been pushed? Neither, medical investigators concluded. He'd gone sleepwalking, and his stroll took an unfortunate turn.

"The autopsy showed that there were significant abrasions along this individual's back, which showed that he fell straight down," notes Michel Cramer Bornemann, an expert on sleep problems who is codirector of the Minnesota Regional Sleep Disorders Center in Minneapolis. "Suicide victims don't fall straight down. They jump." Moreover, the man had been barefoot yet had not been deterred by the roof's layer of sharp stones. "Sleepwalkers don't sense pain; the sensory neural pathways are essentially off-line," says Cramer Bornemann, who was brought in by a family lawyer investigating the hospital's suggestion that the death was a suicide.

Sleep Forensics

Cramer Bornemann heads up Sleep Forensics Associates, a group that lawyers and law enforcement officials have turned to when investigating crimes that may be explained by a sleep problem. Since they've been together—just over two years [as of May 2009]—he and his two colleagues have fielded approximately 150 requests for case evaluations, some from as far off as New Zealand. Murder, sexual assault, DUI [driving under the influence], child abuse, and "suicide" are just a sampling of crimes they've encountered. All have been suspected of involving sleepwalking, sleep driving, or sleep sex, among other so-called parasomnias—inappropriate, unwanted behaviors that arise during sleep. (About one third of those case referrals involve the alleged influence of the sleep aid Ambien, he says.)

While Cramer Bornemann is noticing an increasing need for the group's input on court cases, he explains that it exists primarily to conduct scientific pursuits. These sleep-disorder cases provide an excellent window into the realm of parasomnias, he notes. Sleep Forensics Associates' approach, he said, isn't unlike that of animal-behavioral researchers who study primates in the wild, hoping to learn which behaviors are genetically determined and which are under conscious control.

Bizarre Sleep Behaviors

Cramer Bornemann tracks every case, every call that comes in, collecting data so that years from now, perhaps in a decade or so, patterns might start to emerge that illuminate the physiologic mechanisms that underlie these bizarre sleep behaviors. "It's an attempt to see the breadth and depth of what's out there," says Sleep Forensics teammate Mark Mahowald, director of the Minnesota Regional Sleep Disorders Center and a professor of neurology at the University of Minnesota Medical School. So far, what's out there has proved "extraordinary," he marvels.

"Millions of Americans have some type of behavioral abnormality [during sleep], a parasomnia," says sleep medicine specialist Carlos Schenck, the third member of the Sleep Forensics group and a professor of psychiatry at the University of Minnesota Medical School. People have climbed out windows, driven for miles, and had sexual affairs in their sleep; they punch, kick, curse, and binge-eat in their sleep. Some of the strangest examples can be found in Schenck's books, *Sleep* and *Paradox Lost*, where he details stories—mostly his patients'—like that of the woman who dreamed she was cooking for a dinner party and awoke at 6:30 a.m. to find the table fully set and the meal ready. And that of the woman who woke to find she had sliced up her cat on a cutting board, the girl who sleepwalked to the top of a 130-foot crane without rousing, and the man who nearly snapped

> **FAST FACT**
>
> A recently defined sleep disorder is sleepsex (or sexsomnia) which means sexual behavior during sleep that a person does not remember after waking. Often the acts are things the person would not do while awake and may be upsetting or even harmful to his or her partner.

his wife's neck as he dreamed he was deer hunting with only his hands as a weapon.

Bizarre sleepwalking behaviors can lead to serious injury or death. **(Getty Images)**

"If This Went a Little Bit Further..."

"You don't have to extrapolate very far to connect what we see on a routine clinical basis weekly to saying that 'if this went a little bit further, this could easily have resulted in violent or injurious behavior with legal implications,'" says Mahowald.

Consider the experience of Ron Voegtli of St. Louis. Asleep, he'd fly out of bed, sometimes two times a night, and snap into "protective mode" against perceived intruders. He'd grab a knife or baseball bat and race around the house, often shrieking, while his wife and young kids stayed in their bedrooms. Never did he behave like that while awake.

"I always thought about . . . the possibility . . . like, what if I would have hurt my wife or one of my kids or something. I wouldn't be able to live with that," says Voegtli, now 63. "That's why I never had a gun in the house." In 1989, Schenck diagnosed Voegtli with sleepwalking and sleep terrors—frightened, hyperaroused behavior during sleep—and prescribed a nightly dose of an antipanic drug called clonazepam (Klonopin), which has cured his long-standing sleep problem.

Sometimes parasomnias do lead to something darker. A young Canadian man, Kenneth Parks, was acquitted for the 1987 murder of his mother-in-law using the

Criteria for Sleepwalking Met by Subjects Studied After Injuring Someone

Criterion	Sleepwalking disorder was ruled out				Sleepwalking disorder was diagnosed	
	Subject 1	Subject 2	Subject 3	Subject 4	Mr. A	Mr. B
Arousals in slow-wave sleep	Yes	Yes	Yes		Yes	Yes
Unresponsiveness during episode	Yes		Yes		Yes	Yes
Amnesia about episode	Yes				Yes	Yes
Confusion after awakening	Yes				Yes	Yes
Clinical distress					Yes	Yes
Not due to substance use			Yes		Yes	Yes
Personal or family history of sleepwalking	Yes	Yes			Yes	Yes
No motivation for attack	Yes				Yes	Yes
No cover-up	Yes	Yes		Yes	Yes	Yes

Taken from: National Heart, Lung, and Blood Institute, National Institutes of Health.

"sleepwalking defense." He arose from sleep one night, drove 14 miles to the house of his in-laws—with whom he was said to be close—and strangled his father-in-law until the man passed out. He bludgeoned his mother-in-law with a tire iron and stabbed them both with a kitchen knife. The woman died; the man barely survived. Parks then arrived at a police station, reportedly confused over what had transpired. Police noted something odd: He appeared oblivious to the fact that he'd severed the tendons in both hands during the attack. That analgesia, along with other factors, including a strong family history of parasomnias, led experts to testify that Parks had been sleepwalking during the attack. Not conscious, not responsible, not guilty.

Part Asleep, Yet Part Awake

What explains such parasomnias? In the '70s, it was believed that all complex behaviors arising from sleep were some form of sleepwalking and that in adults, they were all indicative of serious underlying psychiatric disease. Not so, found Mahowald and Schenck; psychiatrically healthy adults could indeed do strange things at night. "Sleep is not a whole-brain phenomenon," says Mahowald. Neurophysiologic studies of sleepwalkers, for example, have shown that during sleepwalking episodes, brain-wave patterns indicate a state of neither full sleep nor full wakefulness: Part of the brain can be awake while the other part is asleep. In sleepwalkers, the part that's shut down governs judgment, says Schenck. "Their eyes are open, they can negotiate the environment; they can see their car keys, grab them, then go drive an automobile," he says. "The problem is, they don't consider the consequences."

They also don't feel pain. That explains how people can go on barefoot forays in the snow without awakening, even as their skin blackens and blisters from frostbite. "If the part [of the brain] that's awake can generate complex motor behaviors, yet the part that's asleep is the part that's normally laying down memories, monitoring what we're doing, then you have a situation where you can have extraordinarily complex behaviors without conscious awareness," says Mahowald. Like murder.

Related Disorders

And the more closely the doctors examined these complex nighttime behaviors, the more they saw they weren't all forms of sleepwalking. There's REM sleep behavior disorder (RBD), for instance, which affects mostly men, age 50 and up. Unlike sleepwalking, RBD occurs during rapid-eye-movement sleep, the stage where most dreaming takes place. It's also the stage in which people should be paralyzed, a protective mechanism to guard against dream enactment.

The doctors noticed, however, that some people could leave the paralysis of REM sleep and become free to act out their dreams: dreams of running on a football field, then colliding with reality, into a dresser; dreams of diving through a window, then soaring headfirst into a wall. By following a group of their RBD patients, the doctors made a remarkable discovery. More than 75 percent of them went on to develop Parkinson's or Lewy body disease, which causes dementia. They now consider RBD an early harbinger of neurodegenerative disorders. (In other patients, RBD seems to be associated with antidepressant use, Mahowald says.)

Many of the cases coming to Sleep Forensics, of course, will turn out to be "Twinkie defenses," [a famous case in which the defendant claimed too much junk food caused him to commit a crime] without scientific merit, from people trying to get off the hook. And even true parasomniacs can commit conscious crimes—and they have. "That's one of the major challenges for us in Sleep Forensics Associates—to work backwards to evaluate the evidence both in favor of a sleep disorder and in favor of criminal activity," says Schenck. "You can't assume that just because someone has a parasomnia, that's why the crime occurred."

CHAPTER 3

Personal Narratives About Sleep Disorders

Experiencing Hypnagogic Hallucinations

**Mike Bremner, interviewed by
Mason Anderson-Sweet**

In the following viewpoint Mason Anderson-Sweet interviews his friend Mike Bremner, who has sleep paralysis with hypnagogic hallucinations. (Although both of them use the term "night terrors," the sleep disorder described is not the same as the one doctors call by that name.) Bremner describes what he feels and sees and how terrifying these experiences are. At first he believed something was actually being done to him, but since it began happening frequently he has become aware, even while paralyzed, that the hallucinations are not real, and he simply waits for the episode to end. Anderson-Sweet is an editorial intern at *Vice* magazine.

I don't know about you, but for me, sleep is something of a refuge. Dreams, epic adventures, and wombish nothingness. For my bud Mike Bremner, sleep is something he succumbs to and endures. He has night terrors. . . . [This disorder] has been around for thousands of years. In the dark ages, Europeans believed it was caused by succubi; in more recent times, aliens. The technical, non-made-up, disorder is called hypnagogic hallucinations. It's a form of sleep paralysis coupled

Photo on previous page.
Sleepwalkers need
to be led gently back
to bed to avoid injury.
(Oscar Burriel/Photo
Researchers,Inc.)

SOURCE: Mason Anderson-Sweet with Mike Bremner, "Night Terrors Are the Worst," *Vice*, March 10, 2010. Reproduced by permission of Mason Anderson-Sweet.

with extremely vivid, and reportedly terrifying, hallucinations. The current consensus is that it's most likely a genetic disorder, passed down generation to generation, and predominantly affecting men. Just reading about it gives me the heebie-jeebies. I've got a hard time comprehending what it would be like to have nightmares on a yearly, let alone nightly basis, so I called up Mike to explain.

Mason Anderson-Sweet: When you're going to bed, what's the first thing that happens that tells you "Well, looks like I'm about to have another night terror"?

Mike Bremner: You can't relax as you're trying to get to sleep. Your body shuts down and your mind is still awake. The sleep-paralysis side of it, which is the first stage, is more of a creeping sensation. Once I'm in a deep state of sleep paralysis, I know it's definitely, definitely, gonna happen.

This is already freaking me out.

I start feeling pressure on my body. Sometimes it even feels like there's a snake or something wrapping around my legs, clenching my legs together. Then I see someone in a peripheral view. This is what's known in night-terror speak, as a shadow person. I never see them directly or physically interact with them.

Eeeeeee.

A lot of the time I feel something going over my legs and then, almost every single time, I feel like I'm being pulled out of my bed and dragged around. I feel them clench my wrists and drag me around the floor like a vacuum. I never leave my room. Whenever I make it to the threshold of the door, I usually manage to get enough energy to try and hit the light switch. It's like a safe zone, I guess. As soon as my finger gets near it, I usually dart up out of bed. I never actually flick the switch, but that's

> **FAST FACT**
>
> Sleep paralysis accompanied by hypnagogic hallucinations is sometimes confused with night terrors (pavor nocturnus), which is the medical term for a different sleep disorder that occurs during deep sleep and is usually not recalled after waking.

when the reset comes. I wake up in my bed and I reach for the closest form of light, be it a phone, computer, lamp. Anything I know that I can control.

Phew. Does that mean you're in the clear?

It isn't always a guaranteed "out." Last night my night terrors looped. I woke up and grabbed the cat at the foot of my bed, and at that point in the terror I figured I was fine because I could control myself. I think that I'm actually awake and I'm not. Then, after that, I had the real waking.

Tell me about your shadow person, does it look like someone you know?

All I can really describe it as is a dark, tall figure with an average-build. The only one I've really seen full-on a couple times is, apparently, the most common night terror figure in the world. It's a seductive red head who says, "Tell me you like me." She's standing at the foot of my bed, never making any real contact, just naked and wanting some action. The odd thing is she isn't really ugly, but like the other shadow figures, you are suppose to be scared of her.

The first time it happened to you, what did you think was going on?

It happened to my brother before it happened to me, only not as serious, from what I know, or as often. His was more of an out-of-body experience. He'd yell in the middle of the night that there was somebody in his room with a gun. Which would alert someone, my parents would wake up or something. I'd be completely dormant through the whole thing so I can't really say how bad it seemed.

Does knowing that it's going to happen make the experience scarier?

Actually it's kind of less scary since I can comprehend what's going on. You know how when you dream you don't always know it's a dream, but at some point you do?

Yeppe.

This isn't exactly like a dream because I can't control myself even though I know it's not real. But I can just wait it out. I sit there wondering when it's going to be over. And, like I said, the light-switch thing. I know every time when that happens I'm going to be OK.

Did you ever think it was anything like a ghost or an alien abduction?

Before I got the grasp that it was a regular thing and I wouldn't be harmed by it or anything, I was convinced that someone was actually doing it. As if I was injected with something and that was why I was semi-asleep and couldn't move.

Hypnagogic hallucinations are usually preceded by a period of restlessness during which the mind cannot shut down. (Oscar Burriel/Photo Researchers, Inc.)

What do you think of people who say their night terrors are alien abductions?

Feeling means nothing, you need to have some form of physical evidence. Or an eye-witness. When I have night terrors, nothing changes in my whole room except maybe the sheets are tossed around. As far as those people are concerned, I'd guess that they're not really educated enough about what's going on. Either that or it's for attention.

Is there any way to prevent the terrors, like drinking or smoking weed?

Yeah, when I'm drunk it feels like my mind has slowed down and I don't really think about it. But I only really drink when I can afford it, and I'm not going to pound a bottle of vodka every night just for peace of mind. As for smoking pot, back when I was getting stoned on the reg [regularly] I definitely had less experiences with the terrors. It still happened, but it was not nearly as often. I think the deal is when I'm high and tired, my mind is a lot more calm, so it's easier to relax on in. Again though, I'm not going to start hitting the bong every night. . . .

That sounds awful.

Eh, it's been happening for so long and it's just going to keep happening. Sure I can prevent it tonight, but I know it's going to come back.

Discovering That Sleep Apnea Needs Treatment

Bill

In the following article a man with sleep apnea tells how he ignored it for years, thinking that he was sleeping through the night even though his wife told him that he snored and sometimes stopped breathing. He did not realize that this was the reason he was so tired during the day. Finally during a routine physical he told the doctor about it and confessed that he fell asleep at traffic lights while driving, so the doctor sent him to a sleep specialist. During his sleep study it was found that his case was extremely severe. He started using a device to keep him breathing at night and was amazed by how much better he felt in the daytime. Bill is a patient who told his story to the American Sleep Apnea Association.

I had actually known I had sleep apnea for a number of years; I just didn't do anything about it. My wife would tell me that I stopped breathing during the night and that she would lie awake counting the seconds until I started to breathe again. I thought I was sleeping

SOURCE: Bill, "Bill's Story: It Was a Big Deal After All," American Sleep Apnea Association, 2008. Copyright © American Sleep Apnea Association. Reproduced with permission.

through the night, so I never really gave it a lot of thought. Anyway, what's the big deal? So I snore and stop breathing. At least I'm getting some sleep.

I did know I was often tired by the end of the day—and during the day. If I went to lunch with a group of co-workers, I would usually migrate to the back seat and take a five- or ten-minute nap on the way back from lunch. I would snore the whole ride back to the office. They were amazed that I could go to sleep at the drop of a hat—and annoyed, too, about the snoring.

A few years ago I went for a routine physical, and my doctor asked me at the conclusion if there were anything else she needed to know. I told her I had sleep apnea. She asked me how I knew, and I told her about my wife's account of my sleep habits. She then asked me if I ever fell asleep while driving. I confessed I had mastered the art of taking a quick nap at traffic lights on the way home from work—but I'd wake up before the light turned green. This really got her attention, and she pulled out a business card from her desk for a sleep specialist.

Two Nights in a Sleep Clinic

Several weeks later I found myself checking into a sleep clinic for the first of two evenings. I was wired astronaut-style with a number of electrodes. The individual wires all terminated into a box about the size of a computer mouse which was then connected to a larger cable connected to the recording equipment. (This disconnect feature came in handy later in the evening when it came time to use the restroom down the hall.) I slept in what looked like a standard hotel room. There was a small video camera mounted in the corner of the room on the ceiling (to let the sleep center compare the printout of my breathing—or lack thereof!—with any tossing or kicking in the night). I woke up the next morning, and the technician told me she had been monitoring two patients that night and didn't pay much attention to either of us

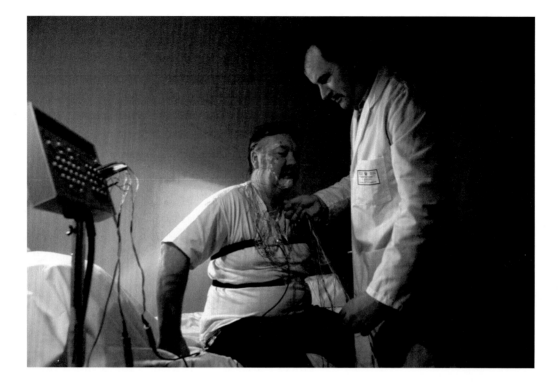

but she thought at a glance I had a pretty serious case of apnea. My actual "log" of activity that documented the entire evening was stored in a computer, and from that the center would generate a report.

The next night I returned, knowing that the diagnostic study must have shown I had apnea, and spent the night in the same room with the same number of electrodes, and the same technician wired me up. The only difference is this time I used an apparatus called a CPAP (Continuous Positive Airway Pressure) machine to keep me breathing; this study would determine what CPAP pressure I needed to control my apnea. I have a full beard, so the tech used the nasal pillows instead of the standard mask as the whiskers on my face probably would have prevented me from getting a good mask seal and would have caused mask leaks. I thus used a "Y shaped" deal that actually fit into my nostrils with round accordion-shaped

Patients sometimes have to spend two nights in a sleep research center in order for sleep apnea to be properly diagnosed. (Veronique Burger/Photo Researchers, Inc.)

"pillows" to route the air into my nose. I spent the night connected to the computer again while the technician was able to control the CPAP machine via remote control and experiment with different settings to see which ones worked best.

Waking up that second morning in the lab was amazing. I felt like a ten-year old who had polished off a pot of coffee. I couldn't believe how completely refreshed I felt! It was truly like the difference between day and night.

A Big Deal After All

A couple of weeks later I was in the specialist's office, and he read me the results of the first night's diagnostic testing. I had experienced an arousal (a mini wake-up call from the brain to resume breathing) *592 times* during the night. This averages out to about 45 seconds of sleep at a time. My sleep was so interrupted, I rarely had any dreaming sleep, so no wonder I remembered dreaming only a couple of times a year! The doctor actually sat straight up in his chair when he got to the blood oxygen levels. A normal level is 95%+. Mine had desaturated, or dropped, to almost 50% during the night. He said, "This is serious. This can kill you." He noted that I had probably been sleep deprived for about fifteen years. You may wonder how anyone could put up with this sort of thing on a nightly basis. The answer is simple: if you don't know it's going on, you don't realize it is a problem. And you become used to the sleepiness and all the other problems sleep apnea causes, and you don't know it's possible to feel any different.

Another week or two went by and I received my bi-level machine. A bi-level differs from a CPAP in that it has two pressures: the higher inhalation pressure keeps me from having apneas, and then the pressure drops to allow me to exhale more easily. (The results of the second

> **FAST FACT**
>
> The Federal Motor Carrier Safety Administration found that 28 percent of the commercial truck drivers they surveyed had obstructive sleep apnea, which causes daytime sleepiness ranging from mild to severe.

night's testing were used to set the machine's pressures before it was delivered to me.) My case was such that the sleep study revealed I would need this type of machine. My machine is also fitted with a humidifier unit that uses distilled water to keep my nasal passages from drying out as I sleep. The whole thing is about the size of a shoe box.

I am pleased to report that after two-and-a-half years, I have had little trouble with my machine. I have traveled all over the United States and have been to nine foreign countries with it. My unit features self-tapping voltage selection—in other words it will run on any available power, all I need is an adapter on the existing power cord to plug into the wall. I have run into two fellow travelers with similar machines at airport security checkpoints and even a store clerk with a machine as I purchased a container for my humidifier unit.

I will admit [that] me with the headgear and the machine is a sight to behold . . . a real "babe magnet." Yet with it, I can be assured a good night's sleep wherever I go. I also don't snore anymore. And my wife is very pleased with that change.

Untreated sleep apnea is a big deal, after all.

GLOSSARY

apnea	A brief cessation of breathing. (*See also* obstructive sleep apnea).
cataplexy	Sudden loss of muscle tone, often causing a person to fall, that is usually triggered by intense emotion. It is considered a diagnostic symptom of narcolepsy.
circadian rhythm	Any body rhythm, such as the sleep-wake cycle, that recurs in twenty-four-hour cycles.
chronotherapy	A treatment technique for circadian rhythm disorders that involves systematically adjusting bedtime by a few hours each day until the desired sleep/wake times are reached.
confusional arousals	Confusion and agitation on waking; common and usually harmless in young children.
continuous positive airway pressure (CPAP)	A device used by obstructive sleep apnea patients that keeps their airways open in order to prevent apnea.
delayed sleep phase syndrome (DSPS)	Inability to sleep during the hours most people do, despite sleeping normally otherwise. Sometimes called delayed sleep phase disorder (DSPD).
dyssomnia	A primary sleep disorder involving abnormalities in the quantity, quality, or timing of sleep.
electroencephalogram (EEG)	The record obtained by a device that measures electrical impulses in the brain.
excessive daytime sleepiness	Chronic severe sleepiness during the day despite getting enough sleep at night. It often indicates narcolepsy, but there are many other causes.
exploding head syndrome	A relatively rare disorder characterized by loud bursts of sound heard in the head as one falls asleep.

hypersomnia	Excessive daytime sleepiness for three months or longer without any known cause; also called primary hypersomnia or idiopathic hypersomnia.
hypnagogic hallucinations	Dreams occurring while falling asleep that are difficult to distinguish from reality and are often frightening. They commonly accompany sleep paralysis and are not the same as night terrors. When they occur while waking up they are called hypnopompic hallucinations.
hypnotic	A medication that induces sleep.
hypopnea	Shallow or excessively slow breathing during sleep, usually caused by partial closure of the upper airway.
isolated sleep paralysis	A disorder in which sleep paralysis and hypnagogic or hypnopompic hallucinations occur in someone who does not have narcolepsy.
insomnia	Difficulty in falling asleep or remaining asleep. It is considered a sleep disorder when insufficient or nonrestorative sleep for many consecutive nights results in impaired functioning during the daytime.
jet lag	Temporary disruption of the body's sleep-wake rhythm following high-speed air travel across several time zones.
Kleine-Levin syndrome	A disorder marked by recurrent episodes of hypersomnia, hypersexual behavior, and excessive eating that occurs primarily in young males.
melatonin	A hormone produced by the pineal gland in the brain that is associated with sleep; sometimes useful in treating sleep disorders.
narcolepsy	A sleep disorder marked by sudden, brief daytime sleep attacks, cataplexy, temporary paralysis, and hallucinations that occur while falling asleep or waking up.
night terrors	*See* sleep terrors.
nocturnal enuresis (bed-wetting)	Involuntary urination during sleep. This is normal up to age five, but is considered a sleep disorder when not outgrown.

nocturnal myoclonus	A sleep disorder characterized by leg cramps or jerking of the legs during sleep, causing repeated awakening; sometimes called periodic limb movement disorder (PLMD).
non-rapid eye movement (NREM) sleep	The four (of five) stages of sleep, including light sleep and deep or slow-wave sleep, during which no rapid eye movement occurs.
obstructive sleep apnea (OSA)	A sleep disorder characterized by recurrent episodes of breathing cessation during sleep, resulting in brief arousals that enable the resumption of breathing but are usually not remembered after waking; sometimes simply called sleep apnea.
parasomnia	A primary sleep disorder involving abnormal behavior or experiences during sleep or the transition from sleeping to waking.
pavor nocturnus	Another term for sleep (or night) terror disorder.
polysomnography (PSG)	Laboratory measurement of a patient's physiological processes during sleep. It usually measures breathing disturbances, eye movement, brain waves, and muscular tension.
primary sleep disorder	A sleep disorder that cannot be attributed to a medical condition, a mental disorder, or substance use.
rapid eye movement (REM) sleep	sleep phase characterized by rapid movements of the eyes under the lids. Dreaming occurs during REM sleep.
REM sleep behavior disorder (RBD)	A sleep disorder in which a person lacks the normal muscular paralysis that occurs during REM sleep and therefore acts out dreams, often violently.
REM sleep latency	The time between the onset of sleep and the onset of the first REM episode.
restless legs syndrome (RLS)	A disorder characterized by crawling, aching, or other disagreeable sensations in the legs that can be relieved only by movement. RLS is a frequent cause of difficulty falling asleep at night.

sedative	A medication given to calm agitated patients. The term is also sometimes used as a synonym for hypnotic drugs.
shift work sleep disorder (SWSD)	A condition caused by an individual's internal clock being out of sync with his or her work schedule.
sleep latency	The amount of time that it takes a person to fall asleep.
sleep onset insomnia	Difficulty falling asleep after going to bed.
sleep paralysis (SP)	Awareness of paralysis at sleep onset or while awakening, often accompanied by hypnagogic or hypnopompic hallucinations. It is a common symptom of narcolepsy but can also occur alone.
sleep-related eating disorder (SRED)	Rapid, involuntary binge eating while partially asleep, often every night.
sleepsex	Involuntary sexual behavior during confusional arousals or sleepwalking, usually not remembered in the morning. Also known as sexsomnia.
sleep study	Overnight evaluation of a patient in a laboratory by means of polysomnography.
sleep terrors (also known as night terrors)	A disorder that involves waking in the night screaming or crying, shaking, and sweating, usually without later recall; not the same as nightmares, nor should it be confused with sleep paralysis.
slow-wave sleep (SWS)	A collective term for stages 3 and 4 of NREM sleep.
somnambulism	Another term for sleepwalking.
somniloquy	Talking during sleep, usually without recall after waking. It is also called sleep talking.

1876 Sleep paralysis—which has been known around the world for centuries—is first described by a scientist, American neurologist Silas Weir Mitchell.

1880 French physician Jean-Baptiste-Édouard Gélineau gives narcolepsy its name and recognizes it as a specific clinical entity.

1913 French scientist Henri Pieron writes a book titled *Le Probleme Physiologique du Sommeil,* which takes a modern, scientific approach to characterizing sleep and which is therefore regarded as a milestone in sleep medicine.

1920s Nathaniel Kleitman, who is regarded as the father of American sleep research, begins his study of the regulation of sleep and wakefulness.

1929 German psychiatrist Johannes Berger demonstrates differences in brain activity between wakefulness and sleep by recording electrical impulses, leading to the development of the electroencephalograph.

1929 Constantin von Economo suggests that a brain site for the regulation of sleep exists. Later in the year, Nobel Prize–winner Walter Rudolph Hess confirms that stimulation in the area he had identified induces sleep.

1937 Through use of the electroencephalograph, Alfred Loomis and his colleagues classify sleep into five different stages.

1950s Gustav Kramer and Klaus Hoffman verify the existence of an inborn circadian (daily) clock, and Colin Pittendrigh studies how it is influenced by temperature and amount of light.

1953 Nathaniel Kleitman and Eugene Aserinsky discover rapid eye movement (REM) sleep.

1957 Kleitman and William Dement define the stages of sleep and establish the relationship between REM sleep and dreaming.

1959 French scientist Michel Jouvet demonstrates muscle paralysis as related to REM sleep.

1961 The Association for the Psychophysiological Study of Sleep, the first sleep medicine organization, is founded. It was later renamed the Sleep Research Society.

1965 Obstructive sleep apnea (OSA) is discovered by scientists in France and Germany.

1970 The first sleep center, Stanford University Sleep Research Center, is established.

1971 Researchers identify genes responsible for the functioning of internal clocks.

1974 The name *polysomnography* is given to overnight sleep studies.

1975 The Association of Sleep Disorders Centers (ASDC), an organization of medical professionals, is established. It is later renamed the American Academy of Sleep Medicine (AASM).

1976 The ASDC establishes a nationally recognized accreditation process for sleep disorders centers.

1978   Mary Carskadon and William Dement create the multiple sleep latency test, which is used to diagnose narcolepsy.

1981   Delayed sleep phase syndrome is first scientifically described.

1981   Continuous positive airway pressure is first used to treat OSA.

1986   The first clear-cut scientific report on sleep-related eating disorder is published.

1987   The World Federation of Sleep Research Societies is founded.

1990   The International Classification of Sleep Disorders, which contains the criteria for diagnosing these disorders, is first published.

1990   Murray Johns develops the Epworth Sleepiness Scale to diagnose sleep disorders.

1993   The US Congress passes legislation to create the National Center for Sleep Disorders Research.

1996   The American Medical Association recognizes sleep medicine as a specialty.

2001   The first human gene involved in circadian rhythms is discovered.

2009   Scientists discover a gene associated with narcolepsy that links it to the immune system, suggesting that it may be an autoimmune disease that produces brain damage.

ORGANIZATIONS TO CONTACT

The editors have compiled the following list of organizations concerned with the issues debated in this book. The descriptions are derived from materials provided by the organizations. All have publications or information available for interested readers. The list was compiled on the date of publication of the present volume; the information provided here may change. Be aware that many organizations take several weeks or longer to respond to inquiries, so allow as much time as possible.

American Academy of Sleep Medicine (AASM)
2510 N. Frontage Rd.
Darien, IL 60561
(630) 737-9700
fax: (630) 737-9790
websites: www. aasmnet.org; www. sleepeducation.com

The AASM is the only professional society that is dedicated exclusively to the medical subspecialty of sleep medicine. It sets the clinical standards for the field and advocates for recognition, diagnosis, and treatment of sleep disorders. The material at its website is for medical professionals, but it maintains another site, www.sleepeducation.com, containing information and a blog for the general public.

American Association of Sleep Technologists (AAST)
2510 N. Frontage Rd.
Darien, IL 60561
(630) 737-9704
fax: (630) 737-9788
e-mail: info@aastweb .org
website: www.aastweb .org

The AAST is a national membership organization representing sleep technologists, whose job it is to assist in the evaluation—including but not limited to polysomnographic studies—and follow-up care of patients with sleep disorders. Besides sections for members, its website contains detailed information about the profession, the nature of the work, and the training it requires.

American Sleep Apnea Association (ASAA)
6856 Eastern Ave. NW, Ste. 203
Washington, DC 20012
(202) 293-3650
fax: (202) 293-3656
website: www.sleep apnea.org

The ASAA is a nonprofit organization dedicated to reducing injury, disability, and death from sleep apnea and to enhancing the well-being of those affected by it. It is active in educating the public about this common disorder. Its website contains detailed information about sleep apnea, a forum, and a directory of resources and support groups.

American Sleep Association (ASA)
website: www.sleep association.org

The ASA is a member-driven public service project that depends on volunteer efforts. Its goal is to educate health-care professionals and the general public about sleep health and sleep disorders. Its website contains information about the various disorders, a newsletter, support group forums, chat rooms, and a searchable directory of sleep labs.

Awake in America
PO Box 51601
Philadelphia, PA 19115-1601
(215) 764-6568
website: www.awake inamerica.org

Awake in America is a national nonprofit organization dedicated to helping people establish viable community education groups to help raise awareness about sleep disorders as well as to provide support and outreach to individuals who have been diagnosed with at least one of the recognized sleep disorders. Its website contains news archives as well as information about the major sleep disorders and about its sleep study relief program, which provides financial assistance to people who cannot afford to have laboratory sleep studies.

Narcolepsy Network
110 Ripple Ln., North Kingstown, RI 02852
(888) 292-6522
fax: (401) 633-6567
website: www.narco lepsynetwork.org

Narcolepsy Network is a nonprofit organization dedicated to individuals with narcolepsy and related sleep disorders. Its mission is to provide services to educate, advocate, support, and improve awareness of this neurological sleep disorder. Its website contains detailed information about narcolepsy and its treatment, a forum, and a directory of resources.

National Center on Sleep Disorders Research (NCSDR)
National Heart, Lung, and Blood Institute
National Institutes of Health
6701 Rockledge Dr.
Bethesda, MD 20892
(301) 435-0199
fax: (301) 480-3451

The NCSDR, a program of the National Institutes of Health, was established in 1993 to combat the serious public health concern posed by sleep disorders. Its website contains a number of fact sheets plus high school curriculum supplement materials on sleep, sleep disorders, and biological rhythms, including a teacher's guide.

National Sleep Foundation (NSF)
1522 K St. NW, Ste. 500, Washington, DC 20005
(202) 347-3471
fax: (202) 347-3472
e-mail: nsf@sleep foundation.org
website: www.sleep foundation.org

The NSF is an independent nonprofit organization dedicated to improving the quality of life for Americans who suffer from sleep problems and disorders. It partners with government agencies and organizations like the Centers for Disease Control and Prevention, the National Institutes of Health, and the Department of Transportation to raise awareness of the importance of sleep and alertness, as well as producing educational materials for media and the general public. Its website contains information about various sleep disorders, a searchable directory of sleep care centers, and a shop for purchasing books and products related to sleep.

Restless Legs Syndrome Foundation (RLS Foundation)
1610 Fourteenth St. NW, Ste. 300
Rochester, MN 55901
(507) 287-6465
fax: (507) 287-6312
e-mail: rlsfoundation @rls.org
website: www.rls.org

The RLS Foundation is a nonprofit organization providing the latest information about restless legs syndrome. Its goals are to increase awareness, improve treatments, and, through research, find a cure for RLS. Its website contains detailed material about the disorder and some patients' stories.

FOR FURTHER READING

Books

Shelley R. Adler, *Sleep Paralysis: Night-Mares, Nocebos, and the Mind-Body Connection.* New Brunswick, NJ: Rutgers University Press, 2010.

Mary A. Carskadon, ed., *Adolescent Sleep Patterns: Biological, Social, and Psychological Influences.* Cambridge: Cambridge University Press, 2010.

Rosalind Cartwright, *The Twenty-Four Hour Mind: The Role of Sleep and Dreaming in Our Emotional Lives.* New York: Oxford University Press, 2010.

Sudhansu Chokroverty, *100 Questions & Answers About Sleep and Sleep Disorders.* Sudbury, MA: Jones and Bartlett, 2008.

L.H. Colligan, *Sleep Disorders.* New York: Marshall Cavendish/ Benchmark, 2009.

Nancy Foldvary-Schaefer, *Cleveland Clinic Guide to Sleep Disorders.* New York: Kaplan, 2009.

Max Hirshkowitz and Patricia B. Smith, *Sleep Disorders for Dummies.* Hoboken, NJ: Wiley, 2004.

D.T. Max, *The Family That Couldn't Sleep: A Medical Mystery.* New York: Random House, 2007.

Judy Monroe Peterson, *Frequently Asked Questions About Sleep and Sleep Deprivation.* New York: Rosen, 2010.

Herbert Ross, *"Alternative Medicine" Magazine's Definitive Guide to Sleep Disorders.* Berkeley, CA: Celestial Arts, 2007.

Periodicals

Howard Beck, "Bowing to Body Clocks, N.B.A. Teams Are Sleeping In," *New York Times,* December 20, 2009.

Lawrence J. Epstein, "The Surprising Toll of Sleep Deprivation," *Newsweek,* July 5, 2010.

Randi Hutter Epstein, "Raiding the Refrigerator, but Still Asleep," *New York Times,* April 7, 2010.

Sarah Kershaw, "Following a Script to Escape a Nightmare," *New York Times,* July 27, 2010.

D.T. Max, "The Secrets of Sleep," *National Geographic,* May 2010.

NewsRx Health, "The Association Between Sleep Disturbances and Reduced Quality of Life Varies by Race," May 23, 2010.

————, "At-Home Sleep Testing Equal to Overnight in a Sleep Lab in Treatment Results," June 6, 2010.

————, "New Study Confirms Positive Effects of Delayed School Start Times," July 25, 2010.

Newsweek, "The Quest for Rest: Millions of Women Suffer from Sleeplessness at Stages Throughout Their Lives," April 24, 2006.

Robert Pinsky, "In the Still of the Night," *New York Times,* July 1, 2010.

Hallie Potocki, "'A Sneaky Sleep Disorder Was Ruining My Life!'" *First for Women,* May 24, 2010.

Roni Caryn Rabin, "No Sex, Please: You're Sleeping," *New York Times,* June 7, 2010.

Andrew Rader, "Nightmares, Dreams and Visualization," *Acupuncture Today,* July 2010.

Laura Sanders, "Sleep Gone Awry: Researchers Inch Closer to Causes, Cures for Insomnia, Narcolepsy," *Science News,* October 24, 2009.

Kevin Wong, "Rest Easy: Inadequate or Poor Sleep Is Associated with Profound Health Consequences," *To Your Health,* May 2009.

INDEX

A
Adolescents/adolescence
  importance of sleep to health of, 36–46
  insomnia in, 54–59
  narcolepsy in, 81–86
  sleep apnea among, 35
  sleepwalking and, 60–66
Alcohol, 59
Ambien (zolpidem), 69, 105–106
American Academy of Pediatrics (AAP), 44
American Academy of Sleep Medicine, 33, 73
American Family Physician (journal), 51
American Journal of Respiratory & Critical Care Medicine, 35
Anderson-Sweet, Mason, 122
Attention deficit hyperactivity disorder (ADHD), 40

B
Barr, Jeff, 50–51
Bates, Betsy, 60
Bed wetting, 93
Benzodiazepine receptors, 69, 71
Benzodiazepines, 70, 109
Bornemann, Michel Cramer, 115–116
Bremner, Mike, 122
Brower, Kirk J., 75, 76

C
CAP (cyclic alternating pattern) analysis, 108, 109
Cataplexy, 22, 85

prognosis for, 28
Central alveolar hypoventilation syndrome, 23
Central sleep apnea syndrome, 23
Chronotherapy, 40–41, 58
Chronotypes, *59*
Circadian rhythm sleep disorders, 23–24, 55, *56*
Cline, John, 54
Cocaine, 78–79
Cognitive-behavioral therapy, 73
Continuous positive airway pressure (CPCP), 44, 51–53, *52,* 129
  bi-level, 130–131
Curatalo, Charles, 50, 53
Cyclic alternating pattern (CAP) analysis, 108, 109

D
Delayed sleep phase syndrome (DSPS), 39–41
Depakote (divalproex), 76, 77–78
Depression, 29
  associated with insomnia, 69–70
  See also Major depressive disorder
Diagnosis, 13–14, *16,* 27
  of narcolepsy, 83–85, 86
Divalproex (Depakote), 76
Dreaming
  brain areas involved in, *91*
  sleep stage associated with, 64
DSPS (delayed sleep phase syndrome), 39–41
Dyssomnias, 20–22